GU00863717

"The Mechanical Handler"
written by BILLY KORTH

First edition

ISBN 978-1-291-50556-6
Copyright © 2013 Billy Korth

This edition published August 2013 in Great Britain
by Estuary Press www.estuarypress.co.uk
Typeset and layout by Estuarine Design
www.madeinessex.co.uk

The Mechanical Handler

"On the wall of the fire station, as in all R.N. fire station garages, there is the biggest red bell in the world. Every morning Air Traffic would test it. Well, without my knowledge my fire crew taped it. On one of my last nights' flying sessions, there I am, half asleep, stretched across a bed, dreaming of better things, when I hear the bell going off. Now, remember at that time of night it is only sounded in an emergency. I ran down the stairs, hopping along as I try to put on my boots. On arrival in the garage, there was all the crew lined up, laughing their little heads off."

FOREWORD

I have been asked many times, "why this title for this collection of stories?"

It is a simple play on words. Those who have served in the Fleet Air Arm will not need an explanation, they will know the term "Mechanical Handler". For those who did not serve, it is a big yellow machine that in the hands of an expert, moves aircraft around the flight deck and hangers. Shakespeare uses the term "rude mechanical" for an artisan, and being as I was, an Aircraft Handler, who am I to go against the Master?

Readers, especially those in the "know," will quickly realise it's about, yes, that loveable creature called the Aircraft Handler, or to give him his character name, "Chockhead".

I am also hoping that this may pull a few heartstrings, possibly get you "chockheads" and "ex-chockheads" reminiscing, maybe relating to these stories; remembering and perhaps saying to oneself, "it sounds as if it could be written about me." Or, alternatively catching the breath and thinking, "there but for the grace of God..."

For many years I have been trying to put pen to paper, to write this story and hopefully get it published. I feel that now, as I approach my more mature years (no comments, gentlemen) it is time to give it one more go.

This not a definitive book about my time in the Royal Navy, but a small collection of stories, or little anecdotes, some of which I hope may make you laugh. They are mainly about me, or what occurred around me. Most of the time it pokes fun at me, and some of the wonderful 'oppos' I shared my Naval life with. After all, we spent a large part of our time laughing, and if you cannot laugh at yourself it would be a sad old world. However is not meant to take the fun out of anyone, and if I have, I apologise in advance.

One more thing. As readers can see I have only used Christian names and the first letter of surnames. This is to protect the guilty - sorry - the innocent. Because if you know the story, you were obviously part of it.

Acknowledgements

I would like to thank Ken Westell, that well-known Aircraft Handler of ill repute, wordsmith and good all-round *bon oeuf* for his valuable help in writing this book.

Dedications

This humble volume is dedicated to those who have served, those who are still serving, and those that have yet to join this great branch, but mostly to those who have 'crossed the bar.'

Moreover, these stories could not have been told without those roughie-toughies and Air Traffic

Softies of the Aircraft Handling branch, whose devotion to their trade and their country over the years has been second to none.

Of course, it has not been possible to mention everyone's name, as I could fill a book. However, to those I have mentioned, I hope I have not shown you in a bad light. I hope you get just as much enjoyment in reading about the past as it has been for me getting the old grey matter going and remembering.

As for the remainder of you, your names and faces will live on in the countless photographs and the tales told of you loveable rogues.

A little homily to end with: "Remember, throughout life you make many acquaintances, but not so many friends. But your real friend will always be THE AIRCRAFT HANDLER."

Personal Dedication

Perhaps most importantly, this book is for the most important person in my life, my darling wife Ruth, as without her support I would not have had the courage to put pen to paper (or to try again.) It is with great pleasure I dedicate this to her. So to the lady that I love, Ruth, I say "thank you darling".

And finally...

If I can only manage to get one book published, it will go to my children and grandchildren, to show them what a little scallywag their father/grandfather was (and possibly still is.) If I am lucky enough to make any money, some will go to Help For Heroes, and some to the Aircraft Handling Association, because without them I could not have written this book.

My Naval History

HMS Ganges	*23/3/1964 – 4/3/1965*
HMS Seahawk	*5/3/1965 – 26/5/1965*
HMS Seahawk	*26/5/1966 – 14/8/1967*
HMS Eagle	*14/8/1967 – 15/1/1969*
HMS Heron	*15/1/1969 – 18/8/1970*
HMS Eagle	*18/8/1970 – 27/2/1971*
HMS Heron	*27/2/1971 – 14/2/1975*
845/846/848 Squadrons	*15/2/1975 – 31/1/1978*
HMS Seahawk	*1/2/1978 – 4/9/1978*
HMS Heron	*5/9/1978 – 7/10/1981*
899 Squadron	*8/10/1981 – 31/12/1981*
Attached HMS Heron/ HMS Hermes	*1/1/1982 – 31/1/1983*
HMS Heron	*1/2/1983 – 18/7/1985*
HMAS Albatross, loaned to RAN	*19/7/1985 – 10/12/1985*
HMS Heron	*11/12/1985 – 7/4/1986*
HMS Royal Arthur	*7/4/1986 – 22/6/1987*
HMS Heron	*23/6/1987 – 7/12/1988*
Terminal leave	*8/12/1988 – 12/1/1989*

Index

1: HMS Ganges (Annex)   13

2: HMS Ganges, The Main Camp   19

3: College Of Knowledge   28

4: The Real Navy   33

5: Second Time Here   43

6: Far East   47

7: Fire Station   55

8: Last Commission of the Big E   86

9: Second Time Around   98

10: Cyprus   102

11: Back Home   107

12: Travelling Out Of A Suitcase   110

13: Round Three: My Spiritual Home   137

14: Yet Another Squadron   141

15: Still At Home   144

16: Leadership School   146

17: Returning Home   148

18: The Final Chapter   152

Glossary of Terms   155

Chapter One

HMS Ganges (Annex)

Why did I decide to join the Navy, and the Royal Navy at that?

From an early age I have always been fascinated by the sea. When I was a young lad growing up in East London, the Second World War was reasonably fresh in everyone's mind, so joining the R.N. (Mob) in 1964 seemed a logical thing to do.

Whilst I was growing up there were stories of the sea being told by my late father and grandfather. Remember that all around us, streets had been flattened. The big build was going on. This was to make way for new housing.

For me and my school mates, playing in these buildings and ruins, our imagination went wild. Where there were front windows still in place, it would be like the bridge of a ship, and we were acting out the part of her captain and crew. We were the stars of the film. At other times it was "Cowboys and Indians".

But mainly we played "British Army against The German Army." Most of all, I think it was listening to all those sea stories from my family about their service in the Navy, and to some extent my older brothers' stories. So perhaps for me, it was like I was reliving their adventures.

I remember Saturday 21st March, my late parents giving me a farewell party before I joined up. It was to be for me, some of my school friends, and of course my family.

The following Monday, 23rd March 1964, my father escorted me to Liverpool Street Station. We were met by this lovely man, or so I thought. He was called a Regulating Petty Officer (RPO, or crusher.) There were a few hundred of us all going to the same destination. He asked for our names, which he ticked off, and duly informed us what platform to go to.

Our train was standing at the platform, the engine quietly hissing steam. For those who remember steam trains, it could sometimes seem to be a three-day camel hike to reach your destination. The carriages were all numbered and on the side were these signs: "NOT FOR PUBLIC USE – TROOP TRAIN".

We must have looked a right sight, all carrying our big brown envelopes and our little cases. It reminded me of those refugees that you see in the war movies. The train was destined for Ipswich - I vaguely knew where that was – and I managed to get myself a seat with a load of other youngsters.

You must remember, we were all fifteen years old and mostly back-street kids. To us, this was going to be one long holiday. (How wrong was I?) To me, it was going to be a joyous occasion. I had never travelled that distance on my own before.

In fact, the journey took about four hours which was not bad. We arrived about lunchtime and were met on the platform by yet more naval personnel, mostly wearing white gaiters with NP armbands on their wrists, and carrying clipboards. I would later learn in my naval career, that if you carry a clipboard, no-one bothered you. Also, these nice men were telling us to get onto the buses which would be taking us to HMS Ganges.

Due to the time we had arrived, we went straight into a big hall - we were informed that this was the gym – where tables and chairs were laid out so they divided the whole hall into little interview rooms. I made my way into a section with the initial to my surname.

There I was met by this nice RPO, who began asking me questions. He asked me to produce three letters. One was from my headmaster (which I still have to this day) and the reason I had to have this letter was I left school before the end of term.

I also had to produce two letters from my father. One was his written permission to join up, and the other informed the Navy that I was a smoker. Then finally, he asked for the letter from MOD (N) informing me that I would be joining HMS Ganges.

He then asked me "do you still want to join up?" After I had given him all the letters, he asked me again if I still wanted to join up, and I was then asked to sign on the dotted line and I did so.

Suddenly, this nice man turned into a snarling, shouting monster with two heads. He then screamed and shouted at me in no uncertain terms, telling me where to go. However, once we got into some sort of order, we were shown to our accommodation in the annex. We were informed that this would be our home for the next six weeks.

Later that evening, after we had been given some working clothes, we had to write the mandatory letter to our parents to say we had arrived safely. Brown paper and string suddenly appeared and we were told to parcel up all our civilian clothes and send them back home as we would not be needing them for at least three months.

After that we were told to go to sleep, or pipe down, as it is known in the navy. You could hear a few of the lads crying. Initially I was a little homesick, and it suddenly dawned on me that this would be the longest time I would be parted from my family. I had done a few Sea Scout camps, but nothing like this. The first two weeks flew past and it seemed for a time, it was all magical. Oh, me of little faith.

Obviously we were to be shown everything Naval. The first was a visit to the "Demon Barber of Shotley." His motto was "anything under your cap is yours, but the rest is the Queen's, the Navy's and mine." So, like those films you see of servicepeople getting a haircut, we all had a crew cut whether we wanted it or not, and oh boy I thought my hair was short. But nothing compared to this.

The next day we visited the naval stores; it was like the movies again. Hat size three, that size, sign here, trousers, this size, sign here, and so on. It went on until we had all our kit.

We then proceeded back to our accommodation, where we were then shown everything about the RN; like how to wash, shave, dress, iron and how to spit and polish our boots and shoes. The funniest thing was trying to embroider my housewife. I have only just lost my housewife (not that one, but a little blue bag which contained needles, cotton and buttons.)

Finally we were taught how to speak Navy, which I believe it is still called "Jackspeak". Shortly after I had joined up I was issued with a suitcase, called a pusser's green, which I still have to this day, 48 years later.

We were all given this number, referred to as an official number. Mine was L080746C. It has changed slightly over the years and by the time I left the MOB it was D080746C . This number would stay with me throughout my career. Another number that I was given would be a ship's book number, mind you that was only used at HMS Ganges.

It was noticeable that there was fifteen Davids, so that was when I decided to use my middle name of Bill, or to some of you, Fat Billy Korth. This was OK when I was with my navy oppos, but got a little bit confusing when I went home, as my late father was called Bill.

Over the next six months we were shown how to march, and make our beds in the naval way. It was like in the films; your sheets tightly tucked in so you could bounce a ball off them. To some of the lads this was a big shock, as at home their mothers did it all. No, not bouncing a ball, but making beds.

So the first six weeks flew past, and the day duly arrived when we had to pack all our kit and proceed over to the main camp. After Sunday divisions and Church Parade, and on this crisp bright morning, we formed up into our division and with the Royal Marine band leading us. "66" Recruitment marched off through the married quarters and into the main gate of Ganges.

This is where the hard work would begin in earnest.

Chapter Two

HMS Ganges (the main camp)

After marching through the camp with the Royal Marines band playing we were informed that our recruitment number would be 66, and that our mess deck was situated in "the long covered way". Over the years, the concrete floor here had become very slippery and shiny. This was caused by all the lads that had passed out before us. They all had hob-nailed boots on (for the uninitiated, boots with studs on.)

Discipline demanded that the middle man of the class had to stop right outside the mess door or you had to do it all again. Hence, when the class was given to order to halt outside the mess, the class leaders had to judge it just right. The whole squad could slide down the road in unison. Looking back, it must have looked quite funny seeing forty young sailors sliding down a slope. The times we had to go round again and do it properly.

If my memory serves me right, there were four divisions to a squadron. During the first few days in the annex, we were introduced to the two Chief Petty Officer instructors. We had to call them "Sir" whilst we were under training.

A few days later we found out their names. The elder one was called CPO(ME) Taylor, and he had more medals on his chest than I had ever seen (see photo 1.) The other was a surly CPO(SE), I am certain his name was Sutton. Our first Divisional Officer was introduced to us, a Lt Commander who went by the name Jim Phillips, if memory serves me well. Because of his love of diving, his nickname was "Deep Sea Jim", he stood about 6ft 6in and was built like a racing split pin.

Over the next year we were introduced to sailing, tying knots and the naval way of doing PT (Physical Training). Way back then I enjoyed long distance running - I used to run for our house at the annual school sports days – and so it came to pass that I was chosen for the steeple chase. Even in those days, I smoked a little, but oh boy, did it take it out of me! For a 15 or 16-year old to be puffing that much. Boy, was I glad I gave up smoking around forty-five years later!

In one respect Ganges was like a boarding school, but with more discipline and the wearing of naval uniforms. We were given instructions in Maths, English and Geography, and of course Naval History and my basic trade training on the Fleet Air Arm (F.A.A.)

I think that the hardest one to pass was the Physical Training. Have you ever tried to hang upside down from a rope and state your official number? Yet another mystery, why is it all PTIs have a voice change when working in the gym?

All these subjects we had to pass before we left Ganges, hopefully to get some advancement later on in our naval careers. On top of trying to pass all these exams, we also had to learn how to iron and fold our kits, so it went into a little locker no bigger than a small chest of drawers, and of course make it so our names could be seen all in a neat and tidy row, and no bigger than one of the naval Ratings Handbook, which we had been given, which was quite a feat.

How strange it is that until this day I still do it the naval way, and when I iron and fold things away, it really infuriates my wife. Mind you, she does let me do all the ironing, as I do such a good neat and tidy job, so I don't know if it's a good or bad thing.

One strange custom they did back then (and apparently they still do) is for you to go into a bunker or darkened room, then you would put on your gas mask and then the instructors would light a CS gas pellet. No problem there, however, once the instructors thought it had burnt for its required time, you took a deep breath, took off your mask and quickly stated your name, rank and number and boy, did you leg it out of the bunker/room.

Once out of there, you would have a big cough. One big problem was you had to stand downwind and let the CS blow out of your clothes and hair. We were told not to rub our eyes, and like most of us, I did not take a blind bit of notice, and immediately rubbed my eyes, which then started weeping like Niagara Falls.

Back then there were plenty of high spirits. Well that's what we called it back then. However, the navy called it skylarking.

One of the many incidents that occurred whilst I was under training was due to smoking. The rule was that nobody could leave the mess deck after 2200. Even those who smoked could not leave the mess. So I and a few others used to pull the blankets over our heads and thought 'ha ha, they can't see us'. But boy, was I wrong. Little did I know that they could see the glow through the blankets. We were spotted by the regulators (naval police) who used to check the messes at night.

In true naval tradition, a suitable punishment was dished out. I was to find out later it was called block punishment. We were informed, or should I say we were "told" that all forty of us were to muster outside. Wait for it, try and picture the scene. We had to wear our pyjamas, hob-nailed boots, oilskins, wearing our respirator and finally carrying our mattress on our backs. The regulators marched us, if you could call it that, to the famous steps that lead from the top of the camp down to the jetties.

They were duly called Faith, Hope and Charity. Oh boy, did someone have a funny sense of humour by calling them that. If my memory serves me right, there was about sixty or seventy steps between the landings, but no matter what time day or night you went there it seemed like a thousand.

We had to double-march to the bottom and then back up to the top and pass the laundry and onto your mess deck. There you were informed that you had five minutes to sort everything out and to be in your bed. It certainly cured me of smoking in bed again.

The famous Ganges laundry! The reason I mention the laundry is this. During the Second World War the Harwich fleet was attacked by German U-Boats and a lot of sailors died. Well, the laundry was the biggest place where they could stow that amount of bodies. In there were drying rails. They were about 20 feet long, they could be pulled out, and there were approximately eight rails per unit. This is where they put the bodies. It was reputed to be haunted, so if you were doing your laundry late at night the slightest sound would get everyone looking around with wide eyes and frowning faces. Collective panic would strike. Suddenly, we would rush around so as we would not be the last one there and had to close up the building.

On yet another occasion we were in the locker room, where all our uniforms were hanging up. It was after lights out, and there we are talking and generally larking about when the shout went out: "Crushers". Ha ha, I thought, I would hide between the uniforms. So I pulled myself up, gathered the uniforms around me and closed my eyes. Oh, little did I know that my hands were showing. I was hanging on for dear life. And as the Crushers pulled the uniforms apart, with those famous words "you can open your eyes now," I knew that once again we all had another little trip to Faith, Hope and Charity.

As we progressed into our year at Ganges, the two things we looked forward to was work ship and two weeks away called sea training.

For work ship I was chosen - or should I say told - that I would be the Senior Rates mess man. Basically this was cleaning up and potato peeling. Even with the potato peeler it took yonks.

The downside was getting up at 0430, to be there early and help the chefs prepare. The upside was that we could help ourselves to the Senior Rates food. For those two weeks, you felt like a proper sailor.

Also during this period you were Captain's Guard, as by then you were the senior course. During those two weeks every day you did the guard in No 8s and on Sunday, wearing our best blues which was for Captain Plaice VC.

I enjoyed the weekends. I found out early whilst at Ganges, that if you volunteered to go canoeing on the fens of East Anglia, you would miss church parade. The things we did to get out of church.

To get to the Fens, you had to transit the busy port of Harwich, so we had to keep close to shore. To pass out from Ganges you had to pass your Naval Swimming Test. This consisted of three lengths of the pool in your pyjamas, staying afloat for three minutes and then diving down to the bottom of the pool to retrieve a solid black rubber brick. To this day I still cannot fathom out why we had to do that and to wear pyjamas.

The officer who took us canoeing was Deep Sea Jim, and whilst we were there we helped clear the Fens. The accommodation, or should I say a big shed, reminded me of the film "The Dirty Dozen," what with the grass you had to sleep on in your green slug.

Also, before you left Ganges we had to go over the mast. To this day it gives me the creeps. As if my ageing memory serves me, the mast was over 300ft high. After a few minutes of climbing, you reached the halfway point. That's where the fun started. You then started to climb out so you were hanging upside down, with the clubs giving you instructions, you would then reach "The Devil's Elbow". Once you had cleared that, it was onto the top, back down the other side. What a relief it was to clear it in one go. (See photo 2.)

Because it was a training establishment you had three weeks leave. The downside was getting up at o'crack of sparrow, a march to the drill shed and then lining up in our ship books number order to be paid. I received the stately amount of £35. Once we arrived home I gave my mum £25, mind you back in them days your money went further.

On one of my first leaves, the creases on my uniform trousers were razor-sharp. I was on a visit to my grandmother's when I pulled up my trousers to sit down, and the top crease on the right side split. Blind panic set in, and my good old grandmother, God bless her, said 'take off my trousers and I will invisibly mend them for you.' No such luck. When I arrived back off leave, even the instructors saw the 'invisible' mend, and to this day I am sure the instructors had x-ray vision - so I paid another trip to the stores to buy yet another suit.

I do remember being paid ten shillings (50p) a fortnight (yes, 50p) and with that you could get one NAAFI pie (now, that *was* a treat), ten cigarettes, two stamps, writing material and still have change. You must remember we only got paid every two weeks, but we did not need anything.

The fortnightly payments continued until about the mid-seventies. By then I was married and my wife got an allocation of money, which we called "handbag pay days", so named as they were given it via the pay office out of our wages, otherwise we might have starved.

The second part was sea training, which consisted of going to HMS Seahawk in Cornwall for two weeks, and they called this establishment RNAS Culdrose. I enjoyed this as, unbeknown to me, when I had finished my year at Ganges I was to be drafted (posted) to this camp for my part 2 trade training.

Whilst we were at Culdrose, two things stood out. One was a day visit to the Naval Dockyard Devonport (Guzz) and we had the day onboard HMS Ark Royal.

That was where I first met the Captain of the Flight Deck (C.F.D.) Ted S was his name, I believe. I remember him saying "I *will* see some of you next year when you join my flight deck."

The Ark Royal seemed so huge, until I saw HMS Vanguard, which was astern of the Ark. Sad to see, as she was waiting to be scrapped. At Culdrose, we were at the Dummy Deck. That was where I would see my first crash on the airfield. It was a Gannet aircraft, which had to land on a foam blanket on the main runway. The aircraft could not get his undercarriage down, however it did land safely. After watching these events and meeting some of the people involved - one of these was a guy called "Shiner W" (AH) - I then realised that I really wanted to be one of those roughie-toughie men.

Before then I had always wanted to be a photographer, as I had all the equipment at home. But alas, it was not meant to be as I failed to get the appropriate marks required. So the day arrived and I and six others got our draft chit to Culdrose, and from then on in, I knew I would be in the navy for a long, long time.

Over the course of the next few months I was to meet up with Shiner many times.

Chapter Three

College of Knowledge: HMS Seahawk, 1965

Together with my oppos I arrived at Redruth station late at night. Remember, we were using steam trains, which took a "three day camel hike" to reach anywhere. A lorry was awaiting us and we were conveyed to HMS Seahawk. After collecting our bedding and being shown to our bunks, it was a very happy sleep.

Our accommodation was called Jellicoe Block. This was situated on one site, but we did our training on another, so every morning after that a Chief Handler by the name of "Tannoy B," used to come into the mess and on the first note of *"Wakey Wakey!"* he would throw a dustbin lid down on the mess deck, with those immortal words of "Stop sleeping!" Boy, what a shock to the system that was every morning - and you had to have your feet on the ground by the count of three.

Next day we did our joining routine, this consisted of getting our joining card, and going around all the various sections and getting it stamped. This was so we were officially on the camp books, and yes, that was when we got that famous ship's book number.

As I stated earlier, one of the people who stood out in my memory was an Aircraft Handler, colloquially known as a "chockhead", named Shiner, whom I had met earlier. One of the biggest lads you would ever see, or to me he was, and so the buzz went around that he was one of the hard-nuts. Between you and me, he was really scared of the dark.

I said "what are they?" He pointed his finger at me and said "come with me, boy". He duly marched me down to the pay office and informed the Wren pay clerk that I wanted my credits. She said "Oh God, not another one". After a few minutes I was given eighty pounds to use for whatever I needed.

Now, to me this was a fortune. As I said before I only received ten shillings a fortnight. This eighty pounds was made up of the odd monies left over, which we all received.

After we left the pay office I asked Shiner if he remembered meeting me before. "Sorry son, no," he replied, then promptly helped himself to twenty quid, as did one of the other guys. With cheeky grins on their faces, they told me that they would return it back to me on their next pay day. By jingo they did, and so the trust was formed. I was to meet up with Shiner many times after that. We spent six months together on the Ark Royal.

Whilst I was at Seahawk the Cassius Clay fight took place. It was due to be televised about midnight. We were still juniors, that is under seventeen, so we needed permission to stay up and watch. We requested and got permission to do this, but lo-and-behold, I fell asleep and missed it completely. Also during this time a handler called Barry "Nobby" H taught me how to play darts. Mind you, I still can't play very well, but that's another story for another chapter.

Like most young sailors, I thought that I was the bee's knees in my uniform. Ginge H and myself trapped a couple of local lasses, they lived in one of the local villages. One of our Leading Hands on the fire station, Taff B, lived in the same village. Around twice a fortnight we went out to see these young ladies, and each payday we would pay him some cash to get fuel to ferry us to and from where the young ladies lived.

Once on our way out, Taff told the "MOD plods" (Ministry of Defence Police) that we were carrying quite a few fire extinguishers in the boot, filled with petrol. My heart sank in my boots, especially when he informed the MOD plods that he was going to be bringing out some more the next night. They just laughed and waved us through. When we went out the next time though the plods searched the truck as usual but could find nothing. Taff turned round and said "Bloody idiots. I told them we had them when I left last night," and as we drove away, we all laughed.

The biggest event of our day was "Rum Issue". Now I was a good little naval rating (or so I thought). I also knew that one of us juniors would be asked to clear up the mess after "Tot Time". I also knew that whoever did it, would get the "sippers", a min tot.

As you true matelots that have gone before know, you only rinse out your tot glass in cold water. Picture this scene. I was given the duty of cleaning the rum fanny (a silver pot with a handle) and all the tot glasses. Both the glasses and fanny were badly stained due to the amount of rum used in them over the years.

Traditionally, cold water is enough. But not for me. I had to clean them out till they shined. Nobody had told me any different. So, in my wisdom I got out the pusser's cleaning paste, and began cleaning, shining, polishing.

While I was daydreaming and cleaning, all of a sudden I heard a cry: "KORTH! What the hell are you doing?"

It was the Leading Hand of the Mess. The air turned blue.

"But, but, but," I said, "what have I done"?

He screamed at me. "You do not clean those glasses or rum fanny! It took hundreds of years to get them that colour. You idiot, Korth, get out and take your pusser's cleaning paste with you, and never touch these glasses again, ever!"

I was then promptly banned from the mess while tots were being issued for the rest of my training, and missed out on a lot of tots.

As the weeks went by we were taught aircraft handling, which was how to move aircraft around a flight deck. This was done on the Dummy Deck, which was basically a vast slab of concrete on the airfield, laid out in the shape of an aircraft carrier.

We also learnt how to put out aircraft and domestic fires at Predanack, the satellite airfield, located on the Lizard peninsula. Incidentally this domestic instruction, designed originally to extinguish any emergency on site, was to come in very handy during the fireman's strike of 1977.

After passing out accompanied by 'Divisions,' we were given our postings, or as we say in the mob, our 'Draft Chit'.

My first draft chit was to HMS Ark Royal. Remember, back in those days I could have gone to any of our five main strike carriers, Eagle, Ark Royal, Victorious, Hermes or Centaur - or the two commando carriers Albion and Bulwark. There was also the Tiger, Lion and Blake Helicopter cruisers plus a vast number of RFAs, so there were a lot of drafts I could have ended up with.

And as I encountered the Royal Navy proper, I was to again meet up with Shiner W.

Chapter Four

The Real Navy: HMS Ark Royal, 1965-1966

The Ark was alongside in Plymouth (Guzz) and I felt now I was in the real navy, and after I had completed my joining routine, now don't laugh lads, I got that well-known ship's book number.

Once I had settled into the mess, yes up he popped, Shiner, and it turned out he was a tractor driver on the watch I was going to.

During flight deck operations at night we had these big lights, which were normally used in the event of a crash on deck. Once the aircraft in the landing pattern got within a certain range of the deck, these lights were switched off. It happened to me a few times that as the lights went off, I was grabbed by this hairy-a***d handler and my arm was being squeezed so hard that my eyeballs nearly popped. I never did find out why Shiner was scared of the dark.

After a few weeks I was on the way to the Far East via the Suez Canal and all points east. I was a junior, under 17½, so naturally I was put into the juniors mess. I think it was 2WZ2. The main thing is I remember about being in this mess was where it was situated.

It was between the main 4.5 armaments on the port side. When they decided to open fire with these guns, the mess shock and the dust that came down from the deck head was incredible.

As we were going through the Suez Canal, you had these traders called gully-gully men come on board . One of these was a local magician, and I was called out to help him. I know what they did was sleight of hand, but he pulled little chickens out of my white front.

I had my first "crossing the line ceremony" (see photo 4.) King Neptune and his little helpers - these were called bears and police, and they had had no resemblance to the real thing - came aboard. Being as it was my first time, I was stitched up – sorry, called forward - and indoctrinated into the ways of the sea by taking part in this ancient ceremony. The white shaving foam and God knows what other foul stuff they put into the water, could only be called rancid. As luck would have it, I was up to date with my injections.

One little incident occurred whilst I was on shore leave. I was in one of the local bars in Sembawang Village in Singapore. Being I was a junior meant that every place we visited I had to be back on board by 2100. It was not like I could hide, as I had to wear uniform. I was about to make my way on board and the bar was crowded.

One of the lads that stood out was Frank N and his nickname was 'Frank the Tank'. As I said, I was about to leave when one bloke was giving the barmaid a lot of hassle and refusing to pay.

Frank stretched his arm out, grabbed this lad by the throat, banged his head on the beam, and said, in a strong Scottish accent, "Pay the lady." Just before he fell down in a big chatty heap, he paid.

Whilst we were out Far East, Singapore was our home port. The main boilers needed cleaning. The stoker's job of course, but volunteers – sorry, working parties - were detailed to assist. The cleaning consisted of the bricks being removed. It took about three days. I never knew soot could get into so many places. With all this soot in my facial orifice I looked like a panda, but someone thought we looked like the chimney sweeps of old.

My seventeenth birthday arrived. Still a junior, I got blind drunk and had to be assisted back on board. I was put into my bottom bunk and the killick of the mess, Mike H was saying "look at that drunken b*****d".

My timing could not have been better. I was violently sick. That wasn't the problem, the problem was *where* I was sick. It shot into the spitkid, caught the lip of it, shot upwards, and landed in Mike's lap. Not recommended. With that he grabbed me and frog-marched me into the showers, put me under a cold shower and scrubbed me with a hard broom until I sobered up.

During the course of this trip I saw my first barrier incident. For a junior it was a sight to behold. It was a Scimitar aircraft that could not get one of his wheels down, so we rigged the barrier.

A PD 150 was a large fire extinguisher on wheels. For any landings I was a glorified barrowboy. I pushed it out on the deck and operated it so the fire suitmen could run it out to the crashed aircraft.

When there was a barrier landing, my safety position was starboard, side forward of the island. I heard the crunching of metal and I started to run out as required. I was grabbed by Mac McC and this aircraft wheel flew past us, bounced and went into the oggin. (see photo 5) I lost a few pounds of adrenalin.

One of the suitmen was Buck J, and most times I was his 150 operator. He had this habit of smoking whilst wearing his fearnought suit. It looked quite a sight, as the smoke was coming out of the little air holes in his asbestos helmet. Mind you, I can think of better ways to kipper yourself.

To get extra shore leave I volunteered to go on a children's party. I know they say 'never volunteer', but as the commission wore on I came to like it.

One of the Flight Deck Officers, called Lt. Bob K, organised a weekend expedition to the Malaysian jungle, to a place called Ulu Tiram where the Gurkhas had their warfare school. So there we are, twelve hairy-a***d chockheads, marching through the jungle. The boss kept reading his map and saying "There should be a plateau here" unbeknown to us. We of course were just following on, carving out things like "KILROY WOZ 'ERE" and "Ark Royal," names and dates. Just out of sight was a Gurkha patrol watching our every move.

We finally reached the boss's plateau. The only problem was that the map he had been reading was a 1943 Ordnance Survey, and this little plateau's little trees were now forty-foot trees. So we proceeded to make our little beds for the night and the boss said "we will do one-hour watches to keep the fire going."

In the early hours of the morning I was poking the fire, when I heard this loud noise. I shone the torch down the path and this huge white thing crossed the path. Me, a coward? You bet I am. I quickly put the watch forewarn and woke my relief early. For the rest of the night I slept with one eye open and my hand on my gollock. (No, not them, a gollock is a big knife.)

For all the lads that were on that first trip into the jungle, I apologise. Whilst we were walking down the trail we had to look out for the person in front of us, in case any leeches got on your skin, and if so, burn them off. As we came out I noticed a big red patch on my left shin area. I lifted my trousers and the leech had been squashed, so I quickly put some sort of medical powder on it to clean it up. I still have the scar today.

Once we came out (see photo 6) the boss asked for a timecheck from the Gurkha, and he wondered why the watch was out of sync.

Before we boarded the transport to go back to the Jungle Warfare School, we walked to the falls. When I first saw it was an idyllic waterfall, like something you would see in the movies. We were only wearing light jungle greens. Once at the side of the waterfall, we took everything out of our pockets and just fell into the cold water. It was great. We quickly dried off. We were strutting around like peacocks, gollocks by our side, jungle warfare ensigns on our shoulders, when a loud shout of "Snake!!" came from the path by the side of the falls.

Being, as we were, true gentlemen, we all raced up there, where a frightened girl was pointing to this huge snake. Again, like the gentlemen we were, we all legged it back down the path.

A small Malaysian boy raced passed us and put us to shame, and in true Indiana Jones style grabbed the snake by the tail, snapped it like a whip and killed it.

We were taken back to the Jungle Warfare school and returned all our equipment. In true military style we were then given a de-brief by a Gurkha officer. He mentioned everything we had done, even down to all our names.

He then called one of the lads out for a little demonstration. He was asked to stand with his back to the bush, he than spoke in Nepalese. Needless to say, we were amazed. Two hands came out from behind him and started to touch him all over. Now, keep it clean - the hands were checking how our boots were laced up. British and her allies do it the same way. Any other way, it's off with your head.

Like all good matelots, whilst the ship was in Singapore I decided to get a tattoo. One of the older lads directed us to Johnny Gurkha's. At the time Johnny was reputed to be the second best tattoo artist in the world.

Well, in we go, me and two others. We all decided to get the same tat. We had it done, left, and then carried on at the nearest bar. Next morning at both watches we were informed that if a tattoo gets infected, we would be charged. Unfortunately Ginge H's tat got infected, but for some unknown reason God shone down on the righteous and I was OK.

One not so good memory was when we went up country. The reason was this. Whilst we were alongside in Mombasa we were told that we could take local leave. I now know where that saying "a three-day camel hike" comes from.

Our leave began with a twenty-four hour steam train journey. One of the best things about the carriage and train, was that we had a servant, which was a novelty. We only had to press the bell and he would arrive with ice-cold Tusker beer. A minor problem was trying to get into your bed when the sheets had so much starch on them.

We finally arrived at Nairobi station. It was a sight to behold. It was like going back in time, as the station looked like a town hall (see photo 7.) We finally got out of the station and were promptly informed that we had another twelve-hour coach journey. Oh, what joy.

On the way to our eventual destination. a town called Eldoret, which was on the Ugandan border, the coach stopped on the Equator (or the line which was painted on the road (see photo 8)

On arrival at this picturesque town, we were billeted with a family on a farm. However, the downside was the ninety-year old granny. She would only speak Dutch Afrikaans, which proved difficult to speak to her as we had to go through her son. It turned out she could speak English quite well, but because of what we did to her ancestors, she refused to.

The day before we were due to return to the ship, the locals had arranged a rugby match. Imagine this, the locals came out all dressed the same, looking very professional. Out from the other end of the hut came Fred Karno's army. We had on every conceivable rig going.

I remember starting the match. The next thing was when I came to about six days later, with tubes coming out of every part of me, or so it seemed. Apparently I had caught a dose (not that one) of malaria, or so I was informed. Incidentally, that was after I had taken those foul Palandrone tablets three times a day. Mind you, the docs on board said it was probably altitude sickness.

Once recovered I had to make that thirty-six hour trip to get back to the ship. I joined her the day before she was due to go to Australia. Drat.

Christmas 1965, the ship was alongside in Freemantle, and our watch was duty. That Crimbo was quite funny, for it was the first time and the only time I had seen this.

As per normal the Captain did his rounds. At that time I was in one of the other handler's mess. The lads had decided to decorate the mess with some festive cheer: toilet paper for "decorations", French letters for balloons and a pair of fireman's boots hanging down from a make shift fire place.

Wonders of wonders, we won a cake for the most original decorations. The killick of the mess brought the cake into the mass and asked who would like a piece. In this mess there was no air-conditioning, but there was a big hurricane fan. Yes, you get the idea. He forced the cake through the rear of the fan. We were finding cake for weeks.

A certain Dave S saw this lonely barrel of beer, decided to keep it company and took it into the mess via the port 4.5 gun sponson. Using a marlin spike he tried to push in the bung, but each time he pushed the bung in the beer would shoot up everywhere, so any container that could be found was purloined to fill up. Great - however, I wonder what questions were asked by the wardroom as this barrel of beer floated gently past the quarterdeck with the beer spouting up, like a whale blowing his blow hole.

On the homeward part of the trip, just before we transited the Suez the Captain decided to have "hands to bathe". No problem, or so I thought. I managed to get into the oggin by jumping in from "four" deck. You came up and, lo and behold, the ship was about half a mile away. You swam back to where the booms were put out with scrambling nets on. You had to grab the net first time, and if not, start all over again. I had just started climbing the net and the wave dropped away. There were two people holding on to my legs.

Needless to say it took me a few attempts, and many bruises later I was back on board. Personally, if someone had shouted "sharks!" we would have all got out quicker.

Chapter Five

Second time here: HMS Seahawk, 1966/1967

I completed eighteen months on the Ark, and the only place I knew was Culdrose, so I put in my preference for Culdrose. I ended up on the 'buffers' party, Seahawk Two, or should I say the 'gophers' party. Over most of the leave periods the galley at Seahawk Two would close down and we had to go about a mile to the main camp. I used to have a meal with the fire pits staff (the old pits.) That is where I found out the difference between mushrooms and toadstools.

To the rear of the pits was a large field where they were abundant. Picture me, if you can, with a basket in my hand. Off I went, mushroom picking. Ben B and I worked under a chief handler, whose name escapes me. Our HQ was the old guard room at Seahawk Two.

Like all good handlers, you always obey the last order, and one day he told us to paint the guardroom outside walls. Well, there we were, painting when this gentleman approached us and asked us what we were doing. You know you want to answer him sarcastically, but the only thing we could reply was "we are painting the building".

What we did not know, was that this chap was a big nob from MPBW, colloquially known as

"The Ministry of Bricks and Sticks". So off he goes and he complains to the Commander. As you know, s**t travels downhill. So the Commander tells the first Lieutenant, who in turn tells our chief that if we did not stop, the whole of Bricks and Sticks would go on strike! So, as only as a Chief Handler can, he orders us to stop. Mind you, that was one way of getting out of painting.

The same two culprits tried something different. At the rear of our building was a now defunct little exercise yard. Being bored, we heard from somewhere how to make bombs. We were throwing these bombs against the wall when our beloved chief caught us and threw a mighty wobbly.

Whilst I was at Culdrose, the Torrey Canyon went aground (see photo 9.) Navy buccaneers were tasked to bomb the ship using certain bombs that we are not supposed to have, but they burnt like oil.

The amount of crude oil that was washed up on the beaches was incredible. When the ship was on fire, this big black cloud of acrid smoke drifted everywhere. I managed to dodge getting down to the beaches and help clear up the oil. If you have not smelt crude oil, you haven't lived.

Down that part of the world was, and still is, the radar unit at Goonhilly Down. It is situated is on coarse grass, and during the summer months it gets very dry - so when a fire starts, it's all hands to the pumps as it spreads rapidly.

Hence we called upon to help out the fire station on the downs; our trusty broom handle with a piece of 4-inch foam hose attached to it, and you beat out the flames. Technical, or what?

Back in the distant past there was this bit of skin PO called Jack C., and he was on the airmanship side of the school. One day I was detailed to help him out. Off we went to Helston to remove a stove from a house.

At the beginning it was OK, then it started to get difficult. There I am, looking up the inside of this chimney using a spanner trying to unscrew a nut, when Jack gave the side of the chimney a whack with a rather large lump hammer.

You know that theory that what goes up must come down? Well, a half a ton of soot came down. I pulled myself from underneath the chimney. Jack said I looked like one of them Victorian chimney sweeps. When we got back to the camp I had to throw away everything I was wearing, and I was cleaning soot out of every orifice for weeks afterwards.

Whilst serving at Culdrose, I had my official eighteenth birthday. Finally, I could drink legally.

I remember staggering along the middle of the road, trying to walk along the while lines, completely failed, and ended up falling over into one of those famous "Cornish" hedges. You know the ones, your side was OK, but the other side was a very large drop.

That is where I was introduced to the local hooch called "Stingo". It is only brewed in the local town of Helston, in a pub called the Blue Anchor and to this day it is still served there.

This strange brew would lift varnish off the woodwork and take the enamel off your teeth. That was the only time that I have tried the local ale; from then onwards I drank the little girl's drink, lager. I still do to this day. No comments, thank you.

You usually had anywhere from six months upwards at an air station, and before my six months were up I had a pier head jump, only because I volunteered.

Yes, I know now that you should never volunteer for anything, but stupid as I was, I did because I was bored. So I joined HMS Eagle about a week before she was due to go to the Far East for the next twelve months.

Chapter Six

Far East, HMS Eagle, 1967/69

This was to be my first time on the "Big E" and, as per normal, there are lots of little things that occurred. Here are a few of the more memorable, and they do say that the happiest ones are the best ones.

When I joined the Eagle, I was a "Hanger Rat", unlike three-quarters of the handlers aboard who worked on the flight deck who were lovingly called "Roof Rats". That episode lasted a few months, and they then informed me that I would be replacing someone who had to go back to his department. He was from the Stokers. During that period, the flight deck party were short-handed, in fact they were short-handed throughout the Navy. Sound familiar?

I was then to become a Flight Deck Firesuitman (see photo 10.) No problem, I thought, however initially I had to take over all his kit. He was six feet tall and very skinny. I was only five foot six and much fatter, and his boots were two sizes bigger. Imagine the sight. There was enough room for two people in this suit.

As with all big organisations, there will be all sorts of characters and over the years there have been many, many, that I remember, with a laugh and a smile. Later I will be writing about one or two of them.

On this trip I learnt to play that ancient game, Mah-Jong (see photo 11) and I still play it to this day. I have succeeded in teaching it to my wife, although she still is not as good as me.

Whilst the ship was in Singapore, I overheard one of the lads, who was going ashore, use that ancient aircraft handler saying: "I am only going on a post card run". I fell for it. I asked him that as he would be back early, would he bring me an egg banjo (a succulent type of sarnie) from the village. I was still patiently waiting for my food when the witching hour came and went, so I got my head down for a snooze. If memory serves me, I was rudely woken at 0300 with a cold egg banjo being shoved up my nose. I think the phrase I used at that time was "go forth and multiply".

As usual, I awoke for breakfast and found this cold egg banjo all messed up in my pit. So, like all good sailors, I kept it for stand easy. Later I wished that I had not, because as stand easy arrived and I unwrapped the package, I saw that decorating the crust was all the print from the newspaper it came in but you know what, guys? It still tasted yummy.

Like all good ships that were stationed out Far East, if you wanted to know anything at all, be it official or unofficial, you contacted the Maggi man. This was a man would appear out of nowhere, to sell you cold drinks. My favourite was the chocolate milk. Still a kid at heart.

The other fount of all knowledge was "Peanuts", the "Cleaner of Crabby Burberry's". Either of these guys would tell you where, what, when. Peanuts would lend you money on your Burberry. In all my career I never saw so many clean and pressed Burberrys.

Another one of these episodes that springs into my mind was New Year's Eve 1967 in Singapore. Due to the heavy monsoon rains, most of the roads leading to the city were flooded. So being very inventive chockheads, myself and a few others - their names elude me - decided to take a taxi to the flooded bit. We then took off our jeans and boots, lifted up the old shirt, and waded through until we got to the dry bit. Then a quick dry off, clothes back on, take another taxi to go some more of the way. This was repeated several times until we arrived in town. On a dry day this trip would take 30 minutes, this time it was over an hour and half. Oh, the joys of being young and in the Navy.

When I joined the Eagle, yet another man stood out. He was known as "Trapper Spinks". To say this guy was different was an understatement. He was a well know matelot of ill repute. I was talking to him one day, and I asked him why he had joined up. It appears him and two friends were caught trying to steal some stuff from a US Air force camp in a place called Attelborough in East Anglia, so the local judge told them to "join up or go to prison". We can guess what happened next. Twenty-odd years later, Trapper was still in the RN.

Whilst we were transiting on the Indian Ocean, we had a Sports Day on the flight deck. This consisted of mainly 'Death Hockey,' which was the flight deck's name for this version of hockey. It was played with what I can only describe as a walking stick, and a puck made out of rope with black tape around it. Little more than a blood sport, it was played to a level of genius by the handlers, a fact well acknowledged by the Wardroom team, who were terrified of meeting them in the final. Apart from the bully-off, which was the only bit that actually resembles the game of hockey, the game rules were made up as we went along, such fun.

It was a hard and fast game. The puck went into the catwalk, or so we thought. In fact it went in between the WT masts and the catwalks. This is a walkway which goes around the flight deck for stores to be stowed. Trapper thought he would retrieve the puck, but surprise, surprise, he missed what he thought was the catwalk and he went straight down into the ocean.

The search and rescue helicopter was launched, and the Dan Buoy dropped - another item used when aiding the rescue of a downed aircraft. It was kept on the Mirror Platform, another deck landing aid. When dropped over the side it emits a signal, enabling the rescue helicopter to locate the crashed aircraft. In this case we were locating a lost and very merry shipmate.

By the time the chopper got to Trapper, he was clinging to the Dan Buoy, singing. Knowing Trapper, he was probably singing a naval ditty but to this day, it was a sight to behold. I will never ever forget it.

Also on this commission were two brothers by the name of Alan and Brian L. Over many months they painstakingly built a replica model of HMS Victory entirely from balsa wood.

Trapper and I were coming back from a meal and as we passed through their mess, he bored two holes into the side of their model. Quick as a flash, he produced some Chinese firecrackers. He put these into the holes, joined the strings together, and pulled them. Just as the two brothers came into the mess, the model exploded into a thousand pieces. For weeks afterwards they were finding bits of the Victory everywhere.

Well, the look on their faces! They were last seen chasing Trapper around the ship and all you could hear was Trapper's cackling laugh as the brothers said "When we get hold of you, oh boy you will pay."

Trapper always had the same routine when he was shaken. You would hear the click of the bunk light going on. Another click as the can spanner hit the top of the beer can. The hiss of the beer can opening, then the sound of the match striking, and finally a wracking cough as he dragged on the first cig of the day.

On this trip we had another helo ditching, no problem as all the aircrew got out safely, the flotation equipment worked, and it floated past the ship. All the general service personnel ran towards the port side and started laughing. The sea boat was launched on the starboard side. The boat was in charge of a Midshipman. He disconnected the launching equipment too soon and the boat started to ship water. Whilst all this was going on, the Fleet Air Arm personnel were laughing our heads off on the starboard side (see photo 12.) The last thing was this middi shouting up to us "tell the bridge", which we never did.

Whilst the ship was in Singapore, Trapper and I and a few others were in Aggie Weston's Sailors' Home. They had the biggest Scalextric set in the world. Trapper, as usual said "watch this". He opened the far window, went back to the other end of the room, got hold of the car handle and pulled the trigger. This car went whizzing down the track, and at the end went straight out of the window and ended up in the swimming pool. The joy of being young and probably a little worse for wear, and yes we were politely asked to leave.

I got away with the monsoon ditch when I was on the Ark, but I got caught out in Singapore.

It was a nightly routine to pile into a taxi and off to Singapore for a few beers. On our arrival in the city, the shout would go up "last one out pays".

One night, good old me thought, "I'll get the jump on you lot," and I exited the cab at speed from the off side. With a shout of "aaaaaaaaah," I ended up covered in what might be called Chinese slime at the bottom of a ten-foot deep ditch. I looked up and there was these grinning faces looking down at me. "You f*****g b*******s," I muttered.

As luck would have it, I was up to date with all my jabs, so I set off towards the nearest ladder and climbed out. After a few pints of Tiger, it was into the heads and through lots of water in an effort to get rid of various things on me, some living, some dead. Touch wood, I did not catch anything.

Hong Kong was another stopoff for memorable runs ashore. During one of these one of the killicks had married a Hong Kong woman. His new father-in-law owned a night club. This killick had not been back in Hong Kong for a few years, so his Chinese relations threw a party in the club to mark his return. What a night, all this good food – and oh, did I mention that all the bar girls were given the time off to accompany us?

Whilst transiting back to Guzz we had a few days in Cape Town. Myself and Happy D (he of the web master) went into this night club. At that time you had to buy the drink before you went into the club and the drink was Cape brandy, another of those drinks that would burn the enamel off your teeth.

After a while, there we were minding our own business, when Happy shouted "Fight!" and at that he stubbed his fag out in my left ear. At the time it did not hurt, but *next morning…!*

Once, safely back in Guzz once more, the ship went into dry dock. Happy, myself and a few others were duty over the Christmas period. When we were duty we would sleep in the Flight Deck ready room as we had to do rounds of the flight deck. Occasionally when we ended up as part of the duty watch you would have to do a fire watch rounds of the dry dock. I still wonder how a ship can catch fire in the bottom of the dry dock, when it's damp everywhere, and above you is a massive 64,000 ship on wooden blocks.

Chapter Seven

Fire station, HMS Heron, 1969-1970

This was one of the happiest periods of my time in the Navy. It was probable the lads that made it so. I joined the Fire Station with the other Roughie-Toughies. We all thought we were the dog's b******s. Our accommodation was on the airfield site behind the Quarter Deck. It was no mean feat to try and look sober as we staggered passed the guard room.

The chief of the section was Gordon P, whose nickname was P3. It was only a small section, it could only hold a bowser and a Land Rover. During the working day P3 used to service Lt Wiggy B's car, so he would wear this brown overall, looking like a school teacher. When he had finished servicing he would always end up with a handful of nuts and bolts and, with a big shrug of his shoulders, he would throw them into the bin. How that car went is still one big puzzle to me.

P3's thing was to try and win the cake for being the best mess on rounds. If you managed this you would be excused rounds next time. One of his bright ideas was to put a fountain and a pond in the TV Room.

It was also a very good time for me as on my twentieth I drew my tot officially. Mind you, I probably owe many of you sippers.

In the NAAFI bar, they had a small bar called the scuffs bar. I was introduced to that ancient game of "spoons". This involved two men facing each other with a little tea spoon in your mouth.

The object of the game was to hit your opponent on the head. After a few games, I wondered what was the object of the game was when *wallop*, I was hit with a sledgehammer. After a few goes, with me getting hit hard, I thought, sod this for a game of soldiers. I called it a night. That was when my opponent produced from behind his back a rather large soup ladle. Over the years I thought, "why should I be the only one to suffer?", so I introduced others to this ancient game.

One Sunday, as usual over the NAAFI bar, it was decided to form a football team which we called the "Scrumpy Shufflers" (see photo 13.) Initially we thought we would play for charity, (whoever she was, ha ha!)

We tended to play the games after a good Sunday DTS. We wore the ship's colours and a variety of boots, trainers and shorts. Our beloved trainer was Bob S, and he would bring with him the magic sponge, a bucket and a mug. The bucket would be full of scrumpy. What a sight he was, wearing his old-fashioned scruffy duffel coat.

The scene was set, and we played the game – well, sort of. One of the lads would go down after a tackle in the opponents half and you would look around. The whole team would be on the ground awaiting a cup of scrumpy. Needless to say, when the powers-that-be heard, we were politely asked to stop.

One of those colourful characters you have on the section was Sippers R. He was on second class, good conduct. In all my time in the mob he was the only one I know who was on it. One of the things he had to do was muster at the guard room in uniform during his off watch time. One Saturday morning we were all in the mess when this RPO came in and shook us all.

Being as it was a weekend, we were all off watch so we did not get up straight away. H then began to shout as only a RP Zero can. He gently informed us that our presence was requested in the fire station garage in ten minutes, wearing our caps, for a warrant reading.

We all thought firstly, "what warrant reading" and, secondly, "have we been caught?" To a man we were all mentally preparing not guilty pleas.

It turned out that Sippers was to be the recipient of the warrant. Unbeknown to us he had been annoying the Wrens on the switchboard. They traced the number, and the result was he was told to pack his kit. He was being discharged from the mob.

With the warrant read the excitement died down, and we went back to bed. A bit later in the day the rumour was that he was given his money for a rail warrant but he spent it at the bar at Yeovil

Junction. When he tried to purchase another rail ticket by saying he was in the mob, the station master rang Yeovilton, spoke to the Duty RPO and the reply was "Sippers who?" The last we heard, he was in the local nick.

Like all good camps, the place to be is the bar. It was here that we got friendly with this RAF chappie. One day it got round to talking about drafting/postings.

This RAF chap wanted to go back to Brize Norton, so being the good little firemen that we were, we gave him some advice. We told him how postings work for us. We explained that to get what you want most, you have to put in for what you want least because they always turn it around; the worst posting first and the one you want last.

The place he did not want was Ben Becular, a radar station way up in the north of Scotland and a place that I was destined to become acquainted with later in my career. A few days later he came storming into the bar cursing and swearing. He then showed us the posting he got. He had been the only volunteer for this post for ten years. We all fell about laughing. At this stage he lost his sense of humour.

Before any airfield opens up in the morning, one of the crew would have to go up to the VCP and collect two Very pistols, six red and six green cartridge flares, plus a pair of binoculars. To come down from the VCP at Yeovil carrying this lot in your arms, you had to bend your head right

58

back and count the steps down. Well, good old Mike R., a leading hand who worked in air tragic, would wait until you were halfway down, when you were concentrating on not dropping anything. Using a loudhailer, he would shout out, telling me to be careful. I would lose my footing, go up into the air with all the equipment around me, and as I landed up in a big heap on the landing, I would look up and this laughing face of Mike's would be looking down. Why was it me he would always get, the b*****d?

On yet another fine day the Admiral's Barge decided to taxi towards 09 Runway before the airfield was open. Crash One, a fire vehicle, was out doing his rounds. It was being driven by Crash E (he knows which one.) Crash One crashed into the barge. Try saying that with these teeth.

I was in Rescue One, the rescue Land Rover, doing our rounds, when air tragic broadcasts "Crash on the Airfield". We all looked at each other and concluded that ATC has made a f***-up. After getting clarification that it was gen, off we went.

On arrival at the scene there was Crash (not the vehicle, running around the 6x6 like a headless chicken. He then he fell down in a chatty heap. Soon after no aircraft was allowed to taxi until the field was open.

During this period at Yeovilton they were rebuilding the gym. They were installing new Parker Ray flooring. This particular weekend was no different from other, that is to say we were a little confused on scrumpy.

Around the sides of our TV room – yes, we had TV back then and no, it was not black and white – were coat lockers. These were ideal for hiding the five gallons of scrumpy in a plastic container, which we drunk out of little pussers tea cups. We always shared the scrumpy with the chefs, as they supplied the food whilst we got the drink. This particular day I went with the duty driver to get more scrumpy.

A voice rang out just as I was climbing back over the crash gate carrying the container.

"Afternoon, Korth". I turned toward the voice and had kittens. There was the fire officer. He had been walking his dog.

I got back to the section and informed Buddy H. who said, "I did not want to be a leading hand anyway", but funnily enough nothing was ever mentioned.

The reason I mentioned the gym was that at this time, they were still using the old-style manual telephone exchange. Later that afternoon they rang us to inform us that there was an exercise fire in the gym.

Blue lights, little devil horns came out of the driver's head. On arrival the usual happened; hoses came out, nozzles were thrown across the brand-new floor. After the exercise there was a debrief by the duty officer, who after giving the duty watch a rollicking, praised us, saying that everyone should be as professional as the fire crew. Little did he know, we were still sociably confused.

The section at this time was going through a transition phase as we were getting some new vehicles, however, we still had our trusted old 6x6 (see photo 14.) On one of those many sunny days it was on the duty runway with Johnny B when air tragic gave out practice crash on the airfield.

Like all good handlers, off we went down the runway. I was the monitor operator. To access the foam monitor you had to get out of the vehicle. It started off, and as the rear of the wagon got level with you, you reached up and grabbed the handle, pulled yourself up onto the running board and climbed up to the monitor.

Yes, true to form, I missed the handle. John shot off down the runway at a great rate of knots. As the vehicle passed me I started running down the middle of the runway waving my arms like Dick Emery and shouting "wait for me," as if he could hear me. As luck would have it, he looked into his mirror and promptly reversed back, and yes, he was in fits of laughter.

Yes John, I *will* relate that other story.

I brought a sit-up-and-beg Ford Poplar from one of the reg staff at the cost of twenty five pounds. Before I could take my test I got drafted, but I managed to sell the car for thirty pounds, so I made a profit.

At the side of the fire station was a painted slot stating "Fire Vehicles Only". On this fine day Ben F was parking the water bowser in this slot when he met some resistance. Ben thought it was the fire crew, tidying the dustbins, and he carried on reversing.

The two things that stand out in my memory were the Lieutenant Commander jumping up and down like a loony, and the deadpan face of his wife, who was still sat in his Rover watching this fire vehicle climbing up the bonnet. Ben got away with it.

One of the routine jobs we had to do was, when the wind changed, we changed the lights around. One day this happened and we left the duty point to proceed up the runway. As usual, there I was, sitting in the back of the Rover with my legs hanging down over the back of the vehicle. As on all naval airfields, arrester wires were in place across the runway and as you passed these you simply lifted your legs.

Once again, readers, you are ahead of me. I did not lift them high enough, was pulled out of the Land Rover and ceremoniously dumped onto the runway. I ended up with a very sore backside.

At the end of the duty runway were phone jacks, into which we plugged a wind-up phone. It was our direct line to air traffic. Many times I left the Rover to answer it. I listened, called out the requirement, then watched as the duty Rover sped off down the runway. I would then have to ring air tragic back, to ask them to send the rescue rover back to pick me up.

By strange coincidence, it seemed that when these little things occurred, Mike R was always about.

Yet another weekend. Why did it always happen at weekends? Why I was always duty?

We received a call to back up the local brigade. They had a rather large Dutch barn on fire, and they required assistance with water. The barn was at the top of Sparkford Hill, by the airfield's transmitters.

I was in a Mark 2 water bowser with Phil McQ. I learnt later that he did not have a drivers' licence. I also learnt something else on that night, that it is advisable to slow down when driving fast over a cattle grid, otherwise you will end up like us; banging from side to side on the bloody thing.

We arrived at the scene with blue lights on horns sounding and the devil horns out of the side of our heads. We were met by the local brigade who were all dressed up, whilst we were wearing just overalls with rolled up sleeves, and welly boots showing white fishermen's stockings over the top.

As we arrived, the farmer's wife was dishing out tea and cream. Unbeknown to us, these were for the firemen who had been there for a few hours. Whilst we were having our cakes, one of the firemen asked us, "don't you wear protective clothing"? "Only when we go to real fires," replied one of the lads. That went down well. The officer in charge then asked, "does that cannon thing work?" He was referring to the monitor on top of the bowser.

After he was instructed on how to use it, he was a happy little soul, directing operations from the bowser. In true naval tradition, we carried on eating cakes and drinking tea.

One weekend Trapper, myself and a couple of other lads decided to have a weekend away on a exped at Cheddar Gorge, to taste the outdoor life (see photo 15.) We duly got all our equipment together, managed to wangle transport, and away we went. We eventually came to this little hill and the transport dropped us off.

We thought we would climb this hill. Wrong - it was like climbing Mount Everest. Finally we found a place to pitch our tent. Then, what goes up must come down, off we went to try and find a local watering hole. We found a place called The Butchers Arms, so for the rest of the weekend that was our home (see photo 16.)

Later on in the summer we went to Cheddar again, this time no climbing. We pitched our tents in the back garden of the Butchers Arms. This was heaven as the landlady would bring us bacon butties each morning.

Over the years Trapper finally got made up to the dizzy heights of killick. Ray F and myself were on his crew. At this time the camp was going through a bit of a change and the fire station was relocated at the South Dispersal. Amongst other things, this meant that the duty crew had to sleep in an small temporary mess.

During the course of the years I have heard people snoring, but Ray could be world champion. He could also have awakened the whole camp. One night, because we could stand no more, Trapper and I picked up his bed with him in it, and placed it outside. For a few hours it was bliss. Mind you, when Ray woke up he was going to kill the whole world.

I know you should never volunteer, but one weekend I did. The section PO, Spike H and I were tasked to Lee-on-Solent to pick up Carl F and then at best speed proceed to Hastings where we would stay for a night. The bed and breakfast place we stayed at was quaint, with low beams and everything. Spike and Carl were turning everything around.

"What port do you come from?" asked the landlord. "That's rather kind of you," replied Spike, "yes, we will all have a port." I tried to keep up with them, however I got a little sociably confused yet again. I woke up with a few bruises on my head, courtesy of the low beams.

In the morning we had to go to a school where the first Sea Lord (the famous one who stopped the tot) was going to land. He was retiring, and as a publicity stunt the Green Parrot (a helo) was going to pick him up. We were to act as a standby fire crew.

A month or so before I was due to join the Eagle, we had another call to help the local brigade.

This time it was approximate six hundred tonnes of rubber, on fire at the Larkhill Rubber factory. The reason for that large amount was due to a rail strike (now, that sounds familiar.)

We got permission from the duty officer and, with a police escort, off we went. Three six by sixes, and oh what joy, we had the two-tones on, blue lights, and horns out of the side of the head. You could see the thick black smoke in the distance as we went down the A303.

When we arrived at the scene you could not have planned it better. All three vehicles swung in, and we all produced foam together. If we had practiced another hundred times we could not have done it.   Spike H, who lived nearby, appeared from nowhere and I believe he was told to go forth and multiply.

During that little stint we used all the stock of foam on the airfield. We had to have an emergency delivery before the airfield could reopen again. Have you every unloaded a forty foot trailer full of twenty-five gallon drums of foam? Not recommended.

Friday 31st July 1970 was a black day in naval history. It was the end of the tot. I did not usually draw my tot at lunchtime, but I thought 'what the hell'.

The airfield shut at normally 1700 and off we went to supper. As we passed into the galley, imagine our surprise when the duty officer asked us whether we had drawn our last tot, as with true naval tradition. We were like rats up a drainpipe and replied "no, sir". I had so many tots that night, I missed my supper and retired hurt early.

Fast forward to next dinner time. Trapper and I were waiting outside the galley, wondering why people were laughing. Then some kind soul informed us that tot finished yesterday. So we skipped lunch, and went over to the bar and got sociably confused again.

At that time the fire crew had a lot of characters. If anything went wrong, you can bet we were involved somewhere.

During that period Simon Dee was one of the biggest stars on TV, and he decided to come to Yeovilton to fly in a Phantom and to judge a talent competition. Everywhere he went that day, no matter what department, he seemed to bump into handlers. The talent show got under way, and a young lad started to sing a traditional folk song, "Old Shep".

Every time he came to the line "Old Shep," the whole front row, which was conveniently made up of handlers, started to howl. As the show and the night went on and the drink was flowing I think more abuse was thrown. Needless to say, we were asked to vacate the premises. No sense of humour, some people.

When the time came for Simon Dee to leave Yeovilton he left with the words "when I send tickets for staff to come to my show, I do not want any handlers there". What a spoilsport.

As was stated earlier the characters were everywhere. One who stands out is J.Q.S. This particular dance night, a Thursday, we were all sitting in a half circle facing the tennis courts with one of the windows open. Before you could say "good morning Chief", J.Q. dived through the window, did a quick roll and landed in a vacant chair. The look of disbelief on the duty committee member's face was a picture. Whether it was because of the reputation of past handlers, or the ones that were serving at the time, when a group of us were in the bar, they were told to keep an eye on us.

It was at the end of term ball and all the Wrens were wearing long dresses. They must have wondered why all the fire station lads were sitting by the Wrens' heads. What they did not know was that we had emptied the two chemicals from a thirty-four gallon foam extinguisher, into the water tank top and bottom of the toilets.

It was like a scene from a Stephen King horror movie, as all this white foam started to appear under the doors and into the main dance area. Wrens were running out, holding their dresses up and screaming.

Yes, readers, we were asked to leave and got banned from the dances. Why is it at times like this everybody gets a massive sense of humour failure?

Another trick especially in the ruperts' heads was to put cling film over the urinals. When they started to do what they had to do, it would splash back onto their trousers. You can imagine the looks they got with their alarming wet patches.

I managed to be on the committee for a few months. Wonder why.

1: HMS Ganges, the first few days

2: The 'Devil's Elbow'

H.M.S. GANGES.

....5/3/45....

Dear ....Keithy....

You have now successfully finished your training at GANGES, and will soon, I hope, be at sea doing the job for which you joined the Navy, and in which all of us at GANGES wish you a happy and successful career.

Remember always, that you belong to the finest Service in the world, respected by all decent people everywhere. To serve in the Royal Navy is more than just a job and you must always do your best, as we have tried to teach you here, to be loyal to the Navy, your ship, and your messmates.

The Navy will give you a chance to see something of the world and in most ships and stations there will be opportunities for sport and recreation of all kinds; take advantage of these whenever you can. You will also have plenty of spare time on board; try and cultivate a hobby to interest you during these periods and so avoid boredom.

The Royal Navy offers great opportunities for advancement and you can certainly get up the ladder if you try. Remember that you will not be chased and persuaded to pass for higher rate. It is up to you. You will have to work on your own and often have to do so when it is so much easier to sitback and take things quietly. Neither will you be nursed domestically; again, it is up to you to pay constant attention to your kit and keep yourself clean and tidy, to the same standards we have taught you here.

Keep out of trouble. The most important thing of all that you should have learnt at GANGES is instant and cheerful obedience. The Navy depends on it. Always remember this. When you are unfairly picked on, when you are very tired, perhaps when you have had a little too much to drink, those are the times - remember - and do what you are told, and if there's good reason complain afterwards. Another important point for keeping out of trouble is to return from your leave on time. In this and in other things you will come across ship-mates who set a bad example, who will probably try to persuade you that there is no point in getting on in the Service; you must use your will-power and refrain from being led astray. Don't for get that it is fairly easy to do your job when things are going right; it takes a man to produce the results when life appears black.

Do not marry too young. Although you will find that you have plenty of spending money as a young bachelor, the financial responsibilities, separations, difficulties caused by moving house, to name but a few drawbacks to early marriages in the Service, make it necessary for you to think particularly carefully before you decide to marry.

Remember the principles of your religion and the vows you have taken here, and try to live up to them.

The very best of luck to you in your career, wherever you may go.

.... Divisional Officer.

B.C.G. Plane Captain

3: On leaving HMS Ganges

72

4: 'Crossing the line' for the first time

5: My first barrier incident

6: Ulu Tiram, Malaysia

7: Nairobi railway station, ca. 1965-66

KENYA
THIS SIGN IS ON THE EQUATOR

EQUATOR

NAKURU—ELDORET ROAD
ALTITUDE 9109 FT

8: The equatorial line

9: The stricken Torrey Canyon

10: Ready for action, HMS Eagle, ca. 1968

11: Mah-Jong

12: Another ditched helo. "Call the bridge!"

13: The 'Scrumpy Shufflers'

14: Fire station, HMS Heron, 1969-1970

15: Cheddar Gorge

16: The Butchers Arms, Cheddar

Chapter Eight

The Last Commission of the Big E
HMS Eagle, 1970 / 1972

Charlie Wines and his henchmen finally caught up with me, and I received a draft chit to HMS Eagle. There was little fatty me and Phil McQ, with all our kit and we travelled to Guzz in Phil's little sports car (not recommended.)

Once I got settled into 4J3 Mess I was to meet various people. I had only been in the mob for six years when redundancies were asked for. My DO, that well-known FDO Sammy H, called for me one day and asked me why I had not put in for it. I informed him that I had not seen all the places I would like to see, plus I was enjoying myself. (I know... *what an idiot* springs to mind.)

When you joined the Eagle, you were given a little blue book which gave you all the relevant details. Both watches of the Flight Deck party would muster on the deck at 0750. The Captain, I.G.W. Robertson, and the Commander would wander up and down the deck until morning colours. The first time they got adjacent to us, the PO of the watch, normally Jim S, would call us to attention, about turn us, and we would all show the Captain the little blue book. For the rest of the commission the book was known as "The Thoughts of Chairman Robbie."

Before any warship goes to sea there is always those two or three joyous days where you have to ammunition ship. As you can imagine with a ship the size of the Eagle, this is no mean feat.

The Flight Deck party was always positioned on the port side aft by the stores hatch in-between the two port 4.5s. Some would be in the gun compartment, helping our fish head friends to store ship.

With not a care in the world, we are throwing these shells and cartridge cases around. That was until a PO, Fish Head, explained to us "that it has been known that the heat from hands has set off those shells. Mind you, it is rare, and if there was an explosion, it would flatten Guzz up to a five to ten mile radius."

We all gulped and handled the rest of the ammo like newborn babies.

Whilst tied up at the coaling jetty, before you carried out sea trials, we would test the catapults with dummy weights and old cars. I think there are more Ford cars in Guzz basin than in the local manufacturers (see photo 18.)

Guzz ratings will know that as you approach towards Plymouth Sound from seaward, you head straight for the Sound then turn towards port, then sharp starboard. Navigation Officers, however, are not all as well briefed as this.

We were returning from sea trials when all of a sudden there was a large bang. It was rumoured you could hear the sound in Plymouth. The whole ship lurched upwards. It turned out that there had been a rock slide and no-one knew about it.

As you can imagine, the buzzes went around the ship as to what had caused this incident. After an initial inspection by the ship's divers, it was found that there was a large hole below the waterline, starboard side. After many more rumours, the command decided to send the ship to Gibraltar dry dock.

Panic set in around the ship. Staff were given time off to go and collect all their tropical kit. I think it was just a ruse to get everyone to collect their tropical kit.

A few days later they removed the Bulwark out of dry dock and we were put in it. Being as we were part of the ship's company, we were ordered to give the seaman department a hand to bring the ship into dry dock. So there we are, down the starboard side by 4J3. The two watch POs came down, Jim S and Bomber B, as well as some unknown fish head PO.

This seaman PO then started to shout all these nautical terms. In true chockhead ways, we looked at him with dumb expressions on our faces. All this nice man had to say was "Lift this rope, pull this one". I think we were then asked not to participate the next time.

Characters seemed to be abundant on this commission. One of them was a throwback to those old sailors of WW2, or should I say he would have fitted in very well. At one time he was killick of the mess. He went by the name of Dennis M. Nothing unusual in that. However, in-between his gas mask case and his life belt kit, he had, all wrapped in plastic bags, fags, book and an assortment of nutty. As he said, "just in case of emergency". As for the underneath of his mattress, this held more nutty than the NAAFI shop.

Dennis was also responsible for painting the forward heads. He did this in the colours of that department; yellow doors with the words "F.D. PARTY".

Another of these colourful chaps was Tex S.

I first came across Tex in the sixties on the Ark. Just before we sailed for the Far East, the flight deck party was having one of those excellent runs ashore. All were merrily walking towards the ship through the darkened dockyard. Out of the gloom emerged these two carriers, the Ark and the Eagle. I think it was the first time in many years that they had both been together. Tex leaves our company and walks up the gangway of the Ark. We all look at each other and wonder what is going on.

About five minutes later, Tex comes down the gangway. Being as we were all nosey b******s, we asked him what had happened. Tex got to the end of the gangway, informed the Q.M. Tex green station card. Off he went into the mess, he switched the light on above his locker (or so he thought) and he realised that not only was it the wrong mess... it was the wrong ship.

Another character/person that I have already mentioned was Mike R. Mike was one of the duty Land Rover drivers on our watch. One of the things he did for the duty watch was, when he landed the night patrol, he would stop and get us a Chuff and Puff. These were rather large pies and a pint of ice cold milk. At 2130 at night, instead of having nine o'clockers, we had that.

Finally, we were all informed that the ship would be doing a world trip before paying off, and that the Big E would then be scrapped.

The day before we were due to sail, two large fridges arrived on the flight deck. The senior storesperson, who confidentially was leaving the mob the day after we sailed, stated, "I want them off this flight deck ASAP". So, like always, we obeyed the last order. They were whisked away from the deck and before you could say "Good morning Chief," they were welded down in our messdeck, a hasp and padlock put on both, and the keys allegedly given to the main Reg office, only to be drawn out when beer was issued.

Whilst we were still doing various sea trials it was decided to have a goodwill trip to Southampton. Why Southampton when Pompey was only across the water? You have heard the old saying "if it moves salute it and if not paint it"?

We entered Southampton with the aircraft ranged in Procedure Alpha.

Whilst we were in alongside our watch was volunteered to paint the flight deck. No problem normally, however it started to rain. We carried on regardless, of course. Were we downhearted? You bet your bloody life.

Hooray, the rain finally stopped, so we wiped up what we could and started repainting the deck when behold, that breed of person, the lesser-spotted "I cannot read" Rupert appears with their ladies in tow. They walked through our wet paint, leaving paint footprints on deck. Up until then I thought they had to read before they went to Dartmouth.

We finally set sail for the Fez. We were informed that one of our tasks would be to bring back the 'Queen's Colours' from Singapore, as it was shutting down due to defence cuts. Sounds familiar.

During one of our visits to Singapore, all the fire suit men went to Simbawang to do some live fire training at this base, with mock up helos. The Chief of this section in Singers was Tom N.

After all the runs had been done and we had had a swim, it was back to the ship for a late breakfast and to top up all the extinguishers.

After breakfast myself and Yanto were tasked to refill the PD150s. This is where confusion reigns. I thought he had released the pressure relief valve, and vice versa. As the valve was released, a big cloud of white powder shot up and went all over the island and the flight deck. I think we may have got away with it if we hadn't decided to start singing "I'm Dreaming Of A White Christmas".

After we had swept up all the residue powder, we spent the next two weeks washing the island.

Whilst the ship was transiting the Australian coast between Sidney and Perth, the ship's tannoy asked me to report to the ship's Reg Office ASAP. Heart in my mouth and thinking "what have I done lately?", I was given a letter addressed "Bill Korth, HMS Eagle, off Australia.

The plot thickened. Even the reggie was intrigued. I opened the letter.

It was from Trapper. Apparently, he had emigrated to Australia about a year previously.

Now, as we all know, Trapper was a likeable rogue. Anybody who knew him will testify to that. Now we all know Trapper, however someone where he worked had put him in charge of distributing blank cheques around the Pacific area for the A.N.Z. banking.

As the ship docked, just as the forward gangway was going out, up came Trapper. Both the First Lieutenant and Uncle Tom (the FMAA) knew him from years gone by.

"What are you doing on my ship, Trapper," asked Uncle Tom. He replied. "It's *Mister* Trapper to you," and then he gave that cackling little laugh. I would have recognised him anyway, as he still had the same tatty herringbone suit on that I last saw him wear at Yeovilton.

He stayed on board the ship for five days, visiting all the mess decks until eventually he was asked to leave by the Josh. That was the last time I saw him as he crossed the bar a few years later.

En route back to the UK via Hong Kong, the flight deck party had had a very good run ashore somewhere, and the next morning we were tasked to chip the flight deck. Chipping hammers in hand, and with a chock to sit on, away we went. But, instead of chipping hammers we all started to use squeaky hammers. The CFD was not amused.

We were alongside in Hong Kong, and we were detailed to bring on firefighting stores. Myself and Ray F were tasked to look after the CO_2 cylinders. This we were doing, when on this humid and sunny day the neck of one of the 12lb cylinders broke off and flew down the flight deck, towards one of the frigates anchored ahead of us. A cry went up: "STOP IT!!" I don't think so. Anyway, it ran out of steam and dropped into the oggin.

Yet another colourful character appears: a young lad by the name of Taff K. In Hong Kong at the time you could order a tailored suit, and it would be made and ready to wear within twenty-four hours. Taff ordered himself one. The next day there he was, wearing a canary yellow three-piece suit, shirt and tie. After we had taken our sunglasses off and picked ourselves up off the floor, he was last seen going ashore.

After leaving Hong Kong, the ship received a distress call from an American ship called the Steel Vendor. She had ran aground on a reef in the South China seas. Our Sea Kings were launched and her sailors were rescued, and all was well with the world.

Later on that evening there was the usual film show in the forward dining hall. What is unusual with that? The film began. It was called Patton. At the front of the show were all these American sailors (see photo 19.) Did they take some stick!

Early on in this chapter I mentioned Yanto. He was my best oppo. We relieved each other as fire suitmen. Same stature, and we both had beards. Sammy H used to shout to Yanto, "Can you do this?", and then wonder why he would not get a reply. Then he would look again and it was me. It worked vice versa too. Poor old Sammy was so confused.

Still en route home when all hell broke loose. Fire alarms going, hands going to emergency stations. It turned out that the liquid oxygen plant had exploded. The handlers helped put the fire out. Mind you, we had some help from the ship.

On another occasion Yanto and I were in the port catwalk. We had been told to bring up all the five-gallon drums of flight deck paint, a heavy task. We decided it would be one for us, and two for Davy Jones. We could not paint the deck for a few weeks. What a shame.

Cape Town, there we were parked alongside. Nearly Christmas, and we were all wishing the next four weeks would go quickly. On this day I was duty watch, nominated as forenoon shore patrol. It was a good number as they are never landed, so come noon I could then go ashore.

I am certain I am jinxed as the shore patrol was mustered, and off we went. We were collected by the South African Police and were informed that we were on route to District Six, as one of our sailors was involved. The police were loading up their elephant guns in the back of the police wagon.

On arrival there was Tex S., laid in the road with his head turned in towards this African and they were both talking to each other in some sort of drunken language. The funny thing is I believe they could understand what each other was saying.

Another colourful person was Slogger S., who was in charge of the fire party. Eagle was armed with Sea Vixen Mk. 2 aircraft. These had their own distinctive ejection seat safety pin, colloquially called a toasting fork. We were short of these pins, so Slogger was asked to get some more from the blacksmiths. The paperwork was put in and I was detailed to collect them. When I saw them I could not believe my eyes. Yes, they were *toasting* forks. Mind you, you couldn't use them for putting into an ejection seat (see drawing, photo 20)

We were minding our own business in Gib for our final time, when this freighter parked on the opposite sea wall went up in smoke. Yanto and I believe that half the ship's company were dispatched to assist in putting out the fire.

On board, both in full fearnoughts on the end of a hose, when, tentatively looking over the top of the bridge was the Rock's chief fireman (see photo 21.) We could not resist it. We turned the hose onto him.

Throughout the commission, the officers would do some strange things for their cocktail parties. The one that stood out was efforts they made in the after lift well. They had it painted pale blue, and when it was flooded, it was turned into a Japanese type lake, even down to the ducks, who were fastened down.

The Eagle has the distinction of having been the last carrier to have a barrier engagement (see photo 22.) On one of the last set of Commanders rounds before we arrived back in the UK, George G was killick of the mess. When the Commander came into the flat outside the mess he asked, "Are you going to paint this flat before we get back"? George replied, "No, Sir, as the ship is being scrapped when we get back". We ended up painting it anyway.

Why is it that you remember silly things, like a group of us sitting by the lockers singing "Me And My Shadow?" Don't ask. The usual suspects were there, Mike R, Dave Mc, Stu Mac, Bob K and of course yours truly.

On this trip I made the fatal mistake of asking the Chinese laundry staff where their 'button crushing machine' was.

Also within a month, I had three Crimbo dinners. One onboard, one with the grippos and finally one at home with my family. To say turkey was off the menu for a while would be an understatement.

We finally arrived back into Pompey on 26th January 1972. There she was de-stored towed to Plymouth and to await The Ark decommissioning.

Chapter Nine

Second time around: HMS Heron, 1972/1975

After a few weeks it was time to leave the Big E and proceed to pastures new, back to sunny Somerset as I got drafted to Yeovilton. Myself and a few others managed to get the Fire Section. One of those was the Association's wordsmith, Ken W.

The section was still at the South Dispersal. At the end of a day shift, the four-tonner we had for our use would pick up all the lads that were not drivers, we would follow the vehicles to a nominated hanger and then we would all proceed over to the living site. On most days the four-tonner would be rocked by the lads and if the driver felt like it he would back it up to the static water tank and the culprits would take an unexpected early bath.

On the section was a young Squeak H. At times he could be gullible. He was coerced into volunteering for the Splash Target Coxswain's Course. There he was with a pilot's helmet on, life jacket and waiting by the static water tank. At the given time he was pulled across the water tank on a board. Oh, I wish I had kept the photos.

Many years later I came across Squeak at another AH Reunion. As I was making my way towards the accommodation, there was Squeak with a white rabbit on an extendable lead. I don't know who was more amazed me, Squeak, or the rabbit.

Near the beginning of the book I mentioned that I was taught to play darts. I still cannot play, but that's another story.

Myself and Ricky H were off duty on a Monday, which was market day in Yeovil. After a few pints we ended up in the Glovers Arms, merrily playing darts together when two lads asked us if we fancied a game of doubles with the usual rules: a pint for the winners and you stay on.

Wonders of wonders, we could not put a foot wrong. We won everything in sight. It was only because we ended up sociably confused that we finally got beat.

Fast forward to Friday and another market day. Off Ricky and I go to the Glovers. The same lads are there. It cost us a mint. We got beat. We could not hit a barn door that day. The two lads then gave us some information. It turned out one was the county champion, and the other was the News Of The World champion. You can't win them all.

Yet another sunny day off, but this time we are all at the Lamb and Lark, a quiet hostelry at the rear of the airfield. After a few hours I went to the heads. When I came back I asked a question (you know, when you think to yourself 'I should not ask this' but your mouth runs away?)

"Who is this Duke of Groose?"

The whole pub erupted and a voice shouted.

"You wally, Korth. It's called Duck or Grouse."

It took many months to live that down.

I believe in 1973 I joined the Security Section. I was on duty with the duty PO and we were doing a drive around the living site. As we approached the wailing wall (explainable later) he turned off all the lights and coasted around the corner. We caught a few people out, they were like rabbits caught in headlights. The first person that was spoken to was George G. As we stopped opposite George, the Duty PO asked what we were doing. George came back with that classic, "I'm necking". The reply was "Put your neck back in your trousers and F**K OFF."

Explanation time. The so called Wailing Wall was so called as it divided up the main camp from the Wrens' quarters. There would be much gnashing and wailing during the course of the nights. I will leave the rest to your imagination.

At this period at Yeovilton I got called "Fat Billy" as I liked my food and beer. Also I could eat pies from the NAAFI wagon, which came twice a day. Nearly every day the NAAFI driver would get caught out by Knocker W, the chief of the Falconry unit. Once the driver had served everyone, Knocker would ask for what he wanted. He would then put this big falcon on the tea wagon shelf and ask for a pie for his bird. It worked every time.

Most weekends must come to an end. We had just completed a Sunday dinnertime session as we had been celebrating my wife's 21st. Myself, Bob K, Goldie K and Joe S and their wives had decided to carry on this party into the evening.

But unbeknown to me and the rest, events in Cyprus were taking a turn for the worse. So there I was, about to leave Bob K's house, when there was a knock on the door. Lo and behold it was Jim S, the section chief. Straight away I said "Not guilty, Jim.", to which he replied, "Pack your kit as you and a few others are going to Cyprus first thing tomorrow". My reply was "you have got to be f*****g joking."

Chapter Ten

Cyprus

Monday morning arrived. We were met at the main gate of the camp by the Master. He gathered us all together and personally took us around all the leaving sections.

The next but last place was the sick bay, for those out of date to get their jabs. Two of the lads, Harry W and Norman O, had a jab in each arm. In fact one of them had two jabs. Did they look a little grey!

After our jabs it was into the pay section to receive some luppins. We were then unceremoniously put on to a bus for Brize Norton. The party consisted of seven of us; Derby A, Yanto Y, Norman O, Harry W, John A and yours truly - and I do apologise for not remembering the seventh name.

Once we arrived at Brize they moved us to South Cerney, a holding unit, as the Army had priority. We met up with others from Culdrose, Portland and a PO and 6 stokers (but we won't talk about them.) Who did I met up with yet again ? Mick R.

Can you believe it, in the corner of this yard was a NAAFI wagon. Nothing strange in that. However, it had been brought out of Cyprus and it contained duty-free beer. HM Customs had decreed that the beer could not leave the yard. We could not disappoint HM Customs, so we had a few beverages, bought some for the journey out, and all was well with the world.

Typical services. We were told that we would not be flying out until tomorrow. So off kit and a quick change into shorts and flip-flops as the sun was shining. How wrong. We got called early so, gathering everything together again, off we went for our eight-hour flight. Oh, what joy.

This was my first flight in a Hercules. In this one was two armoured cars and a jeep, some RAF chaps, and us mateloes. After an uneventful flight we were on our final approach to RAF Akrotiri. The WO Loadmaster starts counting heads. Two attempts later and a confused look appears on his face. With a scratch of his head, he starts to speak into his microphone. Just as the wheels are about to touch down, the missing person pops his head out of one of the armoured cars. No, for a change it was not me, but Harry W. The look on that loadmaster's face was a joy to behold.

All the handlers from Yeovilton and Culdrose ended up at Dhekelia, which had a small runway where C130s could just land and take off.

When not working, airfield duties we were attached to the 23 Army Fire Brigade, mind you I did not know the army had a fire brigade. This was where I first came across the infamous Green Goddess. The officer in charge was Station

Officer Harry Petty (not bad, eh Mike?) If there was a fire in the Turkish quarters, the Greeks would not go and vice versa, even though they had worked together for donkey's years.

When the airfield was open we positioned the fire vehicles at the end of the runway to stop traffic.

One fine sunny day, we were about to close the road when a Land Rover approached, full of Gurkhas. They were escorting another Land Rover full of troops. Nothing strange, however five minutes later, another convoy appeared. After they had gone, we asked the Gurkhas what was going on. Apparently the road was on British Sovereign Area. The first lot were Greek Cypriots and they were being chased by the Turkish, so the Gurkhas escorted them to the end without their weapons. What a way to fight a war.

On one of those many days we had off, some of the lads decided to have some shore leave in Famagusta, which at the time was being controlled by the UN, and was out of bounds. Did that deter a good handler? Of course not.

There I was, minding my own business, watching the TV, having a little drink. I believe we were drinking some resemblance to brandy, called cockenelly.

Suddenly, coming across the courtyard under its own power, was this cardboard box. A UN patrolman appeared and said, "Where is he?" The cardboard box continued on its way. The patrolman caught up with it and lifted the lid.

These slurred words were heard to come out of the box.

"Shush. I am a tortoise."

The lid went down and it started crawling away. The look on this patrolman's face was a picture. As he walked away he was heard to say, "You matelots will be the death of me". (Remember, George S?)

Whilst on the island some of the lads became friendly with the nurses from BMH. Young Jock D had decided to take a short cut across the valley to get to the bar quicker.

The palm of his hand got badly cut. At the bar one of the nurses produced a sewing kit and promptly stitched him up, which seemed a good idea at the time. No problem or so we thought, as it was doused with copious amounts of brandy to disinfect it. We carried on drinking. No luck for Jock. A few days later he had to go to BMH to have it sorted out as it went septic. He had a lot of explaining to do.

One of the beach bars kept moving in and out of the BSA depending on world events. The only snag was that they would put the roadblock in and, using the cunning of a fox and the ingenuity of the SAS, we just walked down to the beach and back up to the road and into the bar.

Before we went home the Turkish Army had another go at the Cypriots. We were at the section, all stood on top of the roof. Across the plain, in the near distance, you could see the two armies fighting. Up above us there were two Phantoms when, all of a sudden, four parachutes were seen as they had ejected.

The story was these jets had asked RAF Akrotiri if they could land, refuel and rearm. Think the reply was "sorry old chaps, no can do".

Finally, the day came when we flew back. No time to tell anyone. After arriving home I did not have my keys so, being a good aircraft handler, I thought 'we always leave the back window open for the dog.' When I first tried to get in, my normally docile Dalmatian nearly ripped my throat out. I made it a second time and he licked me to death. It surely must be me.

Chapter Eleven

Back Home: HMS Heron

During this period at Yeovilton, the powers-that-be decided to have another airshow, and for the love of me I cannot remember what it was for.

Anyway I am on the highest paid crew on duty. Me and LA(AH2), my driver a NA (AH2) and the third member, a LA(AH3), duly parked by the cross-section of the airfield. Luxurious weather, so it seemed a good idea to do a bit of 'Bronzy Bronzy'. So we stripped down our tops and then our overalls and sat on the top of the Land Rover.

Unfortunately we were spotted by the duty, A.T.C. PO A Ben H, (who later transferred to the RAF) He called: "Rescue 2, Rescue 2".

It takes a few minutes to slide down from the top of the vehicles and answer the radio. In that time every man and his dog in the tower were looking our way. Wings, Little F, SATCO, DATCO, even the duty cook. Here we go, I thought, I am in the s**t again.

In one respect I was glad they did call us. We had only just got dressed when a Sea Fury had an undercarriage collapse as it was trying to do a short turn onto the short runway, so perhaps it saved us.

The following week we all ended up on the Officer of the Day's table. The funniest part of it was when we went on OOD's, the duty Officer was the fire officer, Jack C.

We finished up at the Commander's table to be weighed off. This time the boss had to say, "this is out of character and he has a good kit". Only joking, Jack. Incidentally, I got fined £11. But I s★★t myself as he said, "Korth, I am going to fine you double what I gave the other LH." I gulped, thinking, here we go, two to three hundred quid. I could have jumped over the table and kissed him.

Off we went to town for a few ales. When I questioned them it turned out the naval airman got a £4 fine, the Leading Hand got a £7, and your truly £11. So that did confirm to me that officers cannot count.

An afternoon visit cropped up to the local fire station. Myself and a few lads went into town early and had a few beers. We then went to the fire station and, whilst we were waiting, I asked if I could go on the hydraulic platform. When the platform was at its highest, it was lowered down by a wire that accounted for your weight.

As I was going down I saw Jack and the rest of the lads and I waved, which seemed to be a good idea. No; yet another rollicking.

Whilst writing I stated that I would not like to be drafted to a squadron. It's not that I disliked squadrons, it was always that you live out of a suitcase, however I did get a squadron after a bit of ducking and diving.

This day the chief of the section called three of us in the office, and he greeted us with "who would like a married accompanied draft to Singapore to close it down?" Like rats up a drainpipe, three sets of hands went up.

"Korth, you have a draft to the Ark. Nobby C, you as well." George S went away happy. I managed to swap that draft a few weeks later. I got another draft, this time to the Bulwark, and I swapped that as well.

By now I was convinced that Charlie Wines and his department were out to get me. A final draft came in this time for 846 Squadron, that was not too bad as when I was not on board I would be at Yeovilton.

Chapter Twelve

Travelling out of a suitcase

HMS Heron, HMS Bulwark, 846/848 NAS and various RFAs, 1975/1978

When I first joined 848 at Yeovilton the Chief was Ian T, and we both shared the same birthday in January. Ian once bought me a pint from the CPOS's mess which was next door.

We finally embarked on HMS Bulwark. Once on board I was going about my own business, namely moving an aircraft in the hangar, when I thought I heard 'Hands to Emergency Stations'. I completed the move and went up to the flight deck, just in time to see one of the RFAs pulling away from us, a refuelling derrick spewing fuel everywhere, and with a big tear down the starboard side (see photo 23.) Apparently, we were doing Officer Of The Watch manoeuvres and we got a little too close.

Fast forward a few hours and we tried again. But as we approached the RFA, someone had painted a target on the side of their hangar with the words 'try again'.

One very strange thing that happened was, as we approached the Bermuda Triangle, the officer of the watch piped "We are just entering the Triangle'. Virtually as the pipe died away, one of the squadron helos took off starboard side and ditched in the oggin. Was it fate or malfunction?

For some unknown reason we disbanded as 848 and recommissioned as 846. The new Reg Chief was Spike H, who had been on the fire station at Yeovilton many years ago.

Whilst embarked on the Fearless in the Med, we were en route from Malta to Sardinia. Onboard was a film crew, there to film the last part of "The Spy Who Loved Me".

The director was - how can I put this? - rather a quaint gentleman. The plan was for one of the helos to get airborne and to do some overhead shots of the ship. We, the crew were supposed to be going about our business. As we got onto the flight deck we all looked up at the camera and mouthed 'Hello Mum'. After much stamping of his feet and gnashing of his teeth, the First Lieutenant came onto the flight deck and in no uncertain words told us to act normal or else. Sailors, normal? I don't think so.

On this same detachment we had to go alongside a freighter which was on fire and give assistance. A few months later, I (and the rest of the ship's company) received salvage money. The most surprising thing about this was that She Who Must Be Obeyed knew about it before I got home. I know now the power of the jungle drums.

A yearly exercise for the Booties and the Squadron was called "exercise clockwork" (see certificate – photo 24.) This was held two hundred miles inside the Arctic Circle, so we embarked on Sir Galahad. Our beloved CO stood on top of a chacon and led us in a chorus of Auld Lang Syne, whilst in the background the Northern Lights appeared. Either that or I was more sociably confused than normal.

Once ensconced at The Norwegian Air Force Base at Bardufoss, the normal routine was day-to-day stuff. But one thing they did insist on was that you had to have your bergan packed at all times, especially if you was a driver, and all the side pockets would be full of Mars bars etc, plus some firelighting straw.

The main reason for the packed bergan was at breakfast you looked at the notice board to see if your name was there. If it was, you were off to the exercise area for twenty-four hours.

When we had been counted off, we all went to the camp area. Here we were paired off with someone of our own size, the idea being the two of you could build a basha in your designated area. After we had been given the safety brief, away we went. Bewilderment showed on my face as the staff said, "now remember, don't eat yellow snow".

The last thing was being shown how to shake a chemical stick then break it. A bright coloured light would be emitted. They are common around the fairgrounds now, but back then, they were rare. You would then hang it by the tree where you were going to pee, hence, "don't eat yellow snow".

We began the given task of building our basha. This was done on five feet of snow, then a layer of leaves and bark, covered by a space blanket and finally, on top of that, your green slug.

Whilst you were working you were sweating like nobody's business. You would start by taking off your hat, followed by your jumper, then if you were still hot - but only for the roughie-toughies - you would take off your shirt. I would stop for a fag and quickly put my clothes back on. It was bit like the Hokey Cokey.

After collecting your firemaking stuff, you would build your fire about three feet from where your head was going to be, the theory being that once the other space blanket (a rather large piece of tin foil) is in place, the heat will be reflected back at you and you are warm. Now I know what a turkey feels like. Mind you, when it was time to get your head down, out would come your bobble hat to keep your head warm.

Every two hours, the staff would come along and ask if you were OK. This twenty-four hour stint cumulated next morning, our last task being to build a signal fire which, when ignited, could be spotted by an over flying aircraft (see photo 25.)

Bardufoss could be a picture postcard in other circumstances. Outside the camp was a big hole. This is where locals and service men alike, would learn to ski, sliding down, and then using 'crab style' to come back up to the top, there to begin again. One weekend I asked the booties on the squadron to try and teach me to ski, or something resembling skiing.

Gingerly I am crabbing up this slope, when alongside me these two Norwegian boys appeared. They both smiled and laughed, said something in Norwegian and pushed me over. Down I went, over and over to end up in a big chatty heap. Then it was my turn to speak a foreign language and, in Anglo Saxon, I informed them to "go forth and multiply".

In my time in and out of the mob I have been cold, but this was that week the squadron sent back to Westlands Helicopters in Yeovil to ask permission to fly in minus twenty-six degrees. Yes, that is correct. Minus twenty-six degrees.

One little gem I brought back from Norway: if you live in a house with central heating, you sometimes wake up with a dry throat. The Norwegians said before you get your fat head down, put a glass of water by the radiator and this will not happen. It works.

Whenever the squadron movement order is published, the advance party is always the drivers and the booties of the MAOT.

Yet another RFA and Exercise beckoned. We boarded RFA, once at sea we were informed that we are going to a place called Kyle of Lochalsh, right on the Western coast of Scotland. We had only been there for a few days when the CO cleared lower deck, and informed us that due to a problem in a place called Belize, we had been given a general recall. I would receive another one later in my career.

All the four-ton lorries were hastily loaded. Whilst this was going on, Sea Kings were ferrying spare squadron staff to Prestwick, there to await an onward flight back to Yeovilton by C130.

Our stores party was dwindling all the time. Time wore on, and by about 2000 we finally managed to load all the vehicles, and were ready to leave.

No such luck. Our beloved chief had bogged down a four-tonner, thereby stopping all the other vehicles from leaving. In double quick time we off loaded his lorry, managed to tow it off, and we were ready to go again.

This time the MAOT Land Rovers went first and disappeared into the distance. Halfway down this country lane, surprise, surprise, our beloved chief did it again; he bogged down the same lorry. This time the whole road was blocked. Were we downhearted? Oh, no.

We had no means off contacting anyone as the bootie signallers were long gone. But there were lots of helos overflying our location. It was agreed that we would jump up and down waving our torches (sounds familiar.)

Finally, a Gazelle landed in the field opposite. The situation was explained, and about an hour later a breakdown lorry arrived.

You always like to beat your other squadron. But this time, while we were waiting for the breakdown vehicle they went tanking past and disappeared.

Once en route again, the chief had a brainwave. He decided that in case anyone broke down, we would travel in convoy speed. Oh, what deep joy. Have you ever travelled at forty miles per hour from Glasgow to Yeovilton? It is not to be recommended.

Approaching Carlisle, we were knackered. We persuaded Spike to stop at RAF Carlisle. The only place they could offer us was a hedge behind the guard room.

A nice summer's night, out came the green slugs. Before long it was like the dawn chorus. I have never heard so many different snoring sounds. Oh luxury, a few hours kip and off we went again.

Now it was the long haul of the M6 / M5. We managed to get onto the M5 when one of the vehicles pulled over, so we all followed.

Out of nowhere this police vehicle appeared, giving it large. "You can't stop on my motorway." He could not believe his eyes as twenty-odd bleary-eyed matelots in all manner of dress approached him. Anyway, Spike had a word with him and away he went again.

We set off from Scotland on Wednesday night and arrived at the squadron hangers on Friday at midday-ish. After refuelling all the vehicles, we looked like 'Fred Karno's Army,' all in different rigs, unshaven, and the only thing in common was we were carrying our SLRs. Sorry, that should read "dragging".

The C.O. approached Spike and you could see they were having heated words. The end result was we could go home, but we must ring in at 0800 and afterwards every four hours with our whereabouts. That first shower and sleep at home was heavenly. Later on that weekend we got stood down to normal readiness as the MOD managed to get the Ark to cover Belize.

In 1977 I was detached with the squadron to Northern Ireland, so I managed to miss the earlier part of the National Firemen's Strike. I arrived back, and after a couple of days leave, I was informed that I would be joining a fire crew in Bridgewater. Vic M was the crew chief.

I had not long been at Bridgewater when we got called out to a fruit and veg shop. The owner had gone to serve a customer, forgetting that he had left a chip pan on the heat. Whoosh, up it went.

Approaching the incident, Vic had already informed me to don a B.A. set. As we got out of the Green Goddess, there, already onsite, carrying out a crew visit, was the chief of the section, and the fire officer Danny Mac.

Danny decided that he would be the second B.A. operator, with me leading. Off we trot. We were going up these twisty stairs when in front of me, stretching from one side to the other, was a bare wire. It was too high to step over, so I shouted to Danny that we would go under. Little fatty me made it.

I suddenly heard this loud shout. The wire was live and he got a burn, right across his bum. Nowadays, every time I see him I always ask "How's your bum?" and, in his own inimitable way, he informs me to "go forth and multiply".

The second incident was at the Bridgewater library. We had been called three times. After the third attempt we were successful. That was the easy part. As you know, you must ventilate after every fire. There I am, fireman's axe in my hand B.A. On, and I start to hack away at this black oak door. Up comes this fire officer and says, "in this brigade we turn the door handle and open the door". This story went around the Somerset brigade like wildfire and I ended up infamous.

In 1978 they decided to hold an enormous amphibious exercise in Norway. The squadron was detached to a large amphibian ship of the US called U.S.S. Austin. It took a few days to get to Norway, and the day finally came when we started to disembark. The helos duly landed us in a field and off they went. I looked around. There was only handlers in this field and no-one else. Why us?

Again, they had dumped us in the wrong field. After many hours thinking that they would come for us shortly, darkness approached. We started jumping up and down and waving our torches (sounds familiar.) Finally we managed to attract a helo to land. Apparently this one had been looking for us. When we got to the proper landing site, I was never so glad to see other people.

I went flying in the front seat a few times. I had asked to go flying, and I was informed that we would be taking up some soldiers. I had been briefed up what to expect, but it is still spectacular.

I sat opposite the air crewman who was sat by the door. Suddenly he got up, opened the door, and pointed to a sign on his back - "FOLLOW ME" - and promptly jumped out of the helicopter.

Even though I was briefed, it was still brilliant. Then suddenly the same aircrew man reappears, lifts his head, peers into the rear of the cab and smiles. The helo was only three feet off the ground. A dope on a rope. I rest my case.

17: HMS Eagle, September 1971

18: Coaling jetty, Guzz, ca. 1971

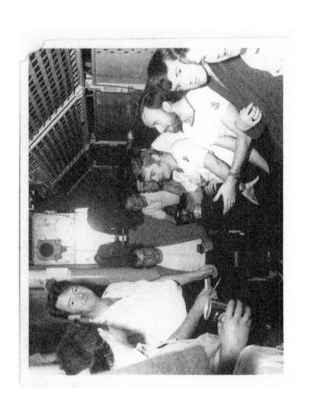

*19: HMS Eagle with assorted
crew from the Steel Vendor*

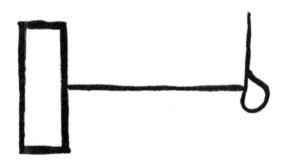

20: The famous toasting fork, see p95

*21: Yanto and I, turning the hose
on Gibraltar's chief fireman*

22: Barrier engagement on HMS Eagle

23: 'Hands to Emergency Stations'

CLOCK WORK

"Talk of the cold
through the parkas fold
it stabbed like a driven nail."

This is to Certify

that _____ D. Korth _____

has survived the hazards of the Arctic and has
lived in habitats designed and constructed by his
own hands.

All this he endured in temperatures to the
depth of -18°C at Latitude 69°N in the year
of Our Lord 1977.

Course Officers { Roy Croston LT RN
                  V. Millward LT (MS) RN

24: Exercise clockwork, Bardufoss, 1977

127

25: Exercise clockwork, Bardufoss, 1977

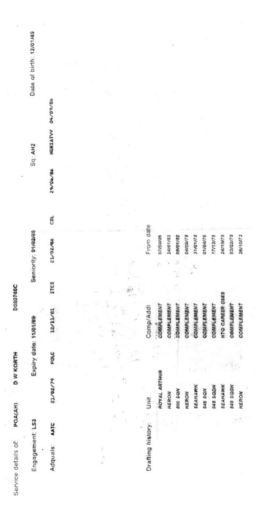

Service details of: POA(AH)   D W KORTH   D080746C

Engagement: LS3   Expiry date: 11/01/89   Seniority: 01/02/88   Sq. AH2   Date of birth: 12/01/49

Adquals: AATC   22/02/79   PQLC   12/11/61   ITC3   21/02/86   CBL   29/04/86   HGRIATVV   04/09/86

Drafting history:	Unit	Comp/Addl	From date
	ROYAL ARTHUR	COMPLEMENT	07/04/85
	HERON	COMPLEMENT	24/01/83
	800 SQN	COMPLEMENT	05/01/82
	HERON	COMPLEMENT	04/09/78
	SEAHAWK	COMPLEMENT	31/01/78
	845 SQN	COMPLEMENT	01/04/76
	848 SQN	COMPLEMENT	17/12/75
	SEAHAWK	HTG CAREER CSES	24/10/75
	848 SQN	COMPLEMENT	03/03/75
	HERON	COMPLEMENT	26/11/73

26: Drafted to Sydney

*27: With the flight deck training
unit at HMAS Nowra*

28: "Spoof" aftermath,
HMS Royal Arthur, ca. 1986-7

H.M.S. Royal Arthur

Staff Senior Rates Mess

Mess Dinner

Friday 18th July 1986

Guests

Commander J.W. Graham R.N.

Warrant Officer J.H. Fletcher

Menu

Pate De Fois

~ ❖ ~

Paupiettes De Sole
Au Crevettes

~ ❖ ~

Chateaubriand Bordelaise
Champignons ~ Asparagus Tips

Darrel Roast ~ Parisienne &
Fresh New Minted Potatoes

Baton Carrots
Broccoli Spears
Aubergines Nicoise

~ ❖ ~

Rhum Baba

~ ❖ ~

Coffee

Soave

~ ❖ ~

Valpolicella

~ ❖ ~

Sandemans
Fine Ruby Port

~ ❖ ~

Chef De Cuisine:
CPO (Ck) Sharp

Maitre De Hotel:
CPO (Std) Walker

29 (opposite) and 30:
My last mess dinner in the Navy

133

*31: "the muddiest and murkiest water
this side of the black stump"*

32: My final draft chit

Telephone :
(0752) 555303

HMS DRAKE
HM NAVAL BASE
DEVONPORT
PLYMOUTH PL2 28G

733/2/1

POA(AH) D W KORTH D080746C
8 Larkspur Crescent
YEOVIL
Somerset   12 December 1988

Dear Petty Officer Korth,

    I am sorry you could not come in to receive this
token of our esteem.

    In wishing you well I echo the Second Sea Lord's
message - thank you for your long service and good luck
for the future.

Yours sincerely,

[signature]

33: Into the next chapter of my life…

Chapter Thirteen

Round Three: HMS Seahawk, 1978 and HMS Heron, 1978/1980

My time at Seahawk this period was very short. I went there to please my wife, only to find that she did not like it, which proves that you cannot win them all.

The second reason was hopefully to complete and pass my 'ones' course. You will not believe who was my instructor. Yes, Mike R. I completed my six months and I received a draft chit back to my spiritual home, Yeovilton.

As usual the first task I had to do was to contact the Married Quarters Officer. I explained what I would like for myself, wife and my two children. Did she throw a massive wobbly? Using the parting words that I could not dictate to her. That got my back up, and I informed her of two things. The first was she worked for us, not the other way round. Secondly, I was prepared to wait for the right accommodation. Her only reply was "I must keep so many houses empty for the Ark Royal." This was in August, and the Ark was not due back unto the end of the year.

I went on a little jaunt and checked out all the MQs. I counted approximately sixty empty houses. I had my ammunition.

I put in an official complaint. The then Josh, Tom W of the sailing programme fame, took me to one side and after explaining to me what could happen, asked if I was prepared to go all the way. He was not worried about me, but he did say "If you get a happy wife and family, you get a happy sailor".

I took my complaint all the way to F.O.N.A.C. and wonder of wonders, the day before I was due to go on Admirals, I was given a house in the area I required. Mind you, they put me through an in muster like you would not believe.

One personal/funny anecdote of this time, mind you it depends what way you see it. I used to travel most weekends from Yeovil to Culdrose. This became uncomfortable because for some unknown reason, I ended up with an ingrown hair at the base of my spine. Off I trot to see the doc. Embarrassingly, the duty doc was a lady. At the time of my appointment, she was also on duty for any emergency on the airfield.

A nice little picture for you. I am lying on the bed with my trolleys down by my ankles with my backside hanging over the bed. The doc puts on a rubber glove and proceeds. (Answers on a post card.)

Then tannoy alert sounds, indicating there is an emergency on the airfield. She unceremoniously pulls her hand out of the rubber glove, and it is left dangling there out of my a**e.

Twenty minutes the doc returns and confronts the scene. I don't know who was more embarrassed. She said, "Oh, I had forgotten about you". Result, I was turned in the sickbay for seven days.

During 1979 I had to do an Air Traffic Control course. Actually I didn't have to, but being as I wanted to go on the MAOT, I had to do this one. I failed the MAOT, and I ended up as an ATC Softie. I did the course with Robbie W. Just imagine, all those young WAAFs and airmen and us two hairy-a***d matelots. Among other things I think we confused the weather man. His favourite saying was "Let's call it a day". Robbie and I would inevitably shout, "OK, let's call it Friday and go on weekend".

Our RAF course Sergeant was built like a racing split pin, and he had this horrible habit of pulling up his trousers. At the end of course PU, even though it was customary to give a pewter mug, we presented a chipped NAAFI tea cup to him. Inside was a pair of braces. To say he was upset for the rest of the night would be an understatement. To stop him crying any more, we gave him his pewter mug before the bar closed.

So I stayed in Air Tragic for a few years and after saving enough Green Shield stamps I was promoted to the dizzy heights of P.O. But to get confirmed in the rank, I had to do a Leadership course at Royal Arthur.

On this course of twenty eight, four were Fleet Air Arm, the other twenty four were submariners. Royal Arthur tradition demanded that you gave your course a leader's name. We all agreed to call ours "Al Capone". That went down with the command. However, when we did some research, it turned out that Capone introduced the first soup kitchen for the unemployed in the USA.

Being as we were the junior course, another tradition was to organise a social evening to welcome all the staff, other courses, and some of the local ladies. Mind you, they came whether you invited them or not.

On the night of the social, a couple of submariners and myself were last seen poking the Captain's chest and saying, "and another thing... I belong to that course". One of the reasons why I did not make CPO.

On another occasion it started to precipitate very hard during one of those group runs through the lovely Wiltshire lanes you did with the PTIs. As one, we all startled to spontaneously sing "I'm Singing In The Rain". The PTIs liked it, and it became our course anthem.

After a while I made it known I would like to leave the Air Traffic side of the branch. In between leaving I received a few rollickings from the Warrant Officer, as I was going around saying "gis a job", until that great day came when the Warrant Officer asked whether I still wanted to leave ATC. I think I bit his hand off.

I could have been in charge of the forward heads but I didn't care. He then informed me I would be joining 899, prior to joining 800 as the Reggie.

Chapter Fourteen

Yet another Squadron: 899/800 NAS 1981/1983

December 1981. I received my draft chit to 800 Squadron, however I had to do a month or so on 899 just to learn some of the routines.

I was relieved on 899 by that well known *Fifteen To One* contestant Pete D. Then I could relieve Lenny S on 800. He spent about two weeks with me, and as far as I know he is now working at the FAA Museum.

As I am sure some of you will recall, we had a little trip away to the Falklands in '82. There have been many definitive books written about the invasion, so I will not dwell on that subject.

The week before all this happened, the C.O. called me into his office and asked if all the next-of-kins were up to date. The following week was Easter, so, as befits any sailors, we had a squadron do.

Half the squadron went on leave after the do. In company with the other half I had to wait until Friday lunchtime. On the Thursday I got my big fat head down early. At 0130 I received the telephone call to get to the squadron ASAP, as there had been a general recall (now, that's familiar.)

Whilst recalling the squadron that morning, I caught a few people out. They were not where they should have been. After much use of the phone, I managed to contact the last person at approximately 1130. As time was tight, I informed him that by the time he arrived back at Yeovilton, we would be on the Hermes. I gave him orders to contact the duty officer on arrival, who would arrange transport to the ship.

Imagine my surprise when he came bowling into the office at 1300. He stated that he came down with his father, but as he was driving down the M5 he was stopped by the police. When he informed them what was going on, they escorted him and others to the camp. Mind you, he did say the only thing that passed them was Concorde.

When we finally arrived back in Pompey, the families were on the jetty waiting. I looked down, trying to see my family. No joy, so back to the mess for another beer. Back and looking down, when suddenly it went quiet. Out of the throng I heard my daughter's voice shouting "Daddy".

We had a few beers on the jetty and then made our way to the coaches back home. The driver had to have a break at Salisbury coach station as he had been up since crack o' sparrow.

So like all good sailors we went to the local pub. There always seems to be one nearby. They had the TV on and they were watching the Hermes returning. The landlady asked us what ship we were from and we informed her 'that one'. The shout went up "the drinks are on me". I arrived home a little worse for wear.

A few months passed and our drafting people informed me that I was going to be drafted to the Falklands. I duly informed my drafting section that at Yeovilton there were other P.O.s who, quote, were 'Barrack Stanchions' and who had not gone down the first time. Yet again, I managed to get away with that one.

Chapter Fifteen

Still at Home: HMS Heron, 1983/1986

This was yet another quiet period in my career. I went from section to section. I went onto the Security Section.

Not much had changed since I was last on this section, except being the PO. I was doing 0700/1900, week off, then 1900/0700, and a week off. So we went on. Two of the chiefs on this section were Dave D and Lemon C. I had served with them both on the Big E in the distant past.

One of the tricks we got up to was on Sunday night we would have a swim to wake ourselves up and then do a 100% ID card check. We would have vehicles backing for miles.

Whilst I am writing I would like to thank Lemon for putting those stones in my hubcaps. Moreover, those kippers he planted near the manifold stank for weeks.

One day I was reading the orders and they were asking for a PO AH to do a swap draft with an Aussie PO. Thinking there would be loads of POs interested, I put in. To my astonishment I got the draft (see photo 26.)

After a three day camel hike I arrived in Sydney. I was drafted to the flight deck training unit at

HMAS Nowra (see photo 27.) The unit was run similar to the one at Portland.

Many incidents remain in my mind. Like all days in Aussie, it was a sunny day. An Aussie handler by the name of Priggy and me were training up some fast patrol boat crews to work with helos. We were dealing with a particularly dismal bunch and all their attempts at lifting personnel had failed. We were minding our own business and instructing at arm's length when Rupert decided to take a hand: "Right, Korth, you show them how it's done."

My initial reply was "No, Sir, as I have an agreement with the sharks; they don't come in my bar and I don't go in their ocean." He had a massive sense of humour failure. The reason that I made these remarks was we were operating in the tiger shark breeding area.

All the time I was in Aussie they were still talking about Pete D and a SE PO.

I arrived back in the UK at Christmas that year. I was informed that I would be the juniors section PO. Great, I could keep my head down do some courses and then leave the mob. How wrong.

I believe I was stitched up whilst I was away in Australia. I got a draft chit to HMS Royal Arthur to be an instructor at the Leadership school. What a shock to the system. I was going back to the real Navy after being away for so long.

Chapter Sixteen

Leadership School, HMS Royal Arthur, 1986/1987

I arrived at Royal Arthur on a Sunday night thinking it would be quiet. Being as it was a leave period, the staff mess was heaving as the courses were using it.

Over the weeks I was joining in with other courses as all those fags and beers was having its toll. The first time I ran a three-miler with the course, I was absolutely f****d. After the course had been dismissed, I went behind the drill shed and mustered my kit.

The one and only Christmas I was there I was duty officer just before Christmas itself. I was in the bar (nothing unusual, I hear you say) when someone suggested a game of 'spoof'.

From what I was told next morning, the concoctions of drinks we had would have killed an elephant (see photo 28.) The evening finished off with a tot and I staggered to my pit. Thank goodness I was not on a squad run. At lunchtime the Chief Wren, who was serving behind the bar, called us over and showed us the spoof drinks list. It was phenomenal. Apparently, this particular list stayed behind the bar until the camp closed.

On a duty weekend there was a mess dinner. I went to the dinner with the other staff members. As we were watching the drummer beating us to dinner, one of my buttons came off. I quickly picked it up, thinking no-one would notice it.

After the dinner, the mess vice-president started fining those that had transgressed. He called my name, for which I thanked him and we had to drink the bottle of port before we could leave the mess (see invitation menus, photos 29-30) and that was my last mess dinner in the Navy.

When you picked up a course, usually a maximum of twenty-four, you could not do your own trade.

My last course was nearly over, and after the last ACL task, the course officer called all the course and me together by the big pond. Before I could do a runner, I was grabbed and thrown into the muddiest and murkiest water this side of the black stump (see photo 31.) Little did they know I had put on all old stuff from stores.

Chapter Seventeen

Returning Home: HMS HERON, 1987/1989

I always classed Yeovilton as my home, so I finally returned to the fire station as a crew chief. This was only going to be a short stint, as the vehicles were changing as well as the manpower required to man the vehicles.

On the crew this time I had a very young lad on the crew. For the love of me I cannot recall his name, but I do remember the incident.

We were on the first floor lazing about. I could hear this persistent scratching sound at the window. So I piped up, "go and check that noise." He opened the curtains. I thought he was going to have a heart attack. Looking through the curtains was Scouse, who was wearing this 'Scream' fright-mask. I don't know about him being frightened, it did wonders for my bowels.

As with all good times, they must come to an end. Due to the shakeup of various things, the manning went down from 6 to 5-man crew. Not too drastic, or so I thought.

Why is it always a sunny day when fate catches you when you are not looking? Being as we were duty crew, we got a call out for a washdown.

As I got out of the vehicle on arrival I shouted "I will do this one". For some reason I decided to hold the hose properly.

The pressure slowly increased, then, without warning, the pressure shot up. The hose was whipped out of my arms and started snaking over the floor.

I jumped up in the air, saying "You are not going to get me." I could not quite jump quite high enough the second time and the hose lug caught me on my right ankle bone. Apparently I did a lovely somersault. If I had been diving I would have got a 9.9 for artistic impression. I was heard to utter those famous words, "this is going to f*****g hurt." I looked up. I was surrounded by these laughing faces looking down at me, all showing sympathy.

From there it was to the local hospital. I ended up on crutches for a few weeks.

One of the other things I am proud of is helping to plan and ride the John O'Groats to Land's End cycle ride for the NSPCC. It was a section thing and it had not been done on that scale before, not by the Navy anyway.

We each did twenty miles or an hour on the bike. When we stopped it was normally at a military unit. One of the stops was RAF Carlisle (déja vu) and our duty chef made mince and tatties. We were eating it and it was very sweet. When we questioned him, he had decided to use cider to cook it in. He was banned from cooking again, and it was back to eating pasties. I enjoyed doing that ride as overall we made £15k for the NSPCC.

When I first joined Yeovilton all those years ago we would night fly around the clock for days. Now it was very rare, so on this night there I am, lazing on one of the beds. The lads well and truly stitched me up.

Every day ATC would do a crash alarm test and it was with the biggest red bell in the world. Well, the lads taped it, so there I am, nearly in the land of nod. When this bell sounds, I am off this bed like a jack rabbit, hopping as I am putting my boots on, and missing every other step on the way to the garage, there to be confronted with the whole of the crew laughing their heads off.

As the months appeared to drag on I had been relieved on the crew and the section chief Dave Mac said 'I only want to see you once a day, to make sure you are alive'. So, grabbing a clipboard, I went wondering around the camp to say farewells to the oppos I had made in nearly twenty years at Yeovilton.

At the last p***-up in the PO's mess. I don't think I thanked Paul for taking care of me. Due to various reasons I was living onboard. There was a fruit machine in this old wooden block. I could not get on it as there was always someone there. This one night I put in twenty pence and the first time around it dropped 200 smackers. Thank you very much!

The last section PU arrived, which was just before Christmas. I was presented with a hip flask and I presented them with a framed photo of the Larkhill Fire. Mind you, I still have the hip flask, but I have upgraded it to a bigger version which I take to the Cenotaph each November. Purely medicinal, of course.

Chapter Eighteen

The Final Chapter

To sum up, in December 1988 I had my final medical. You know the Navy; you were fit when you came in, so you had to be fit to leave. Apart from one little mishap, I was pronounced fit, the mishap was that little cigarette in my ear (thanks Happy.) Off to Haslar, a little operation, and after three days back to Yeovilton.

When I went to Drake Barracks, the record for discharge was 45 minutes, set by Pete D. They asked if I would like to attempt to break it. I declined (see last draft chit, photo 32.)

Once you had completed your routine you were asked if you would like to see the commodore, usually at 1630. I declined that one as well. A few weeks later I received a letter thanking me for my time (see letter, photo 33.)

Throughout these little stories, it may seem as if it was all drink-related methinks - whether it was from boredom or perhaps trying to live up to the name of 'Chockheads' that had gone before.

And so my time came to an end after completing twenty five years for Her Majesty.

I hope some of these stories made you laugh at me, or with me, or just to jog your memories and say, "I remember doing that", or "that was me." Most importantly, you must have a laugh.

I do hope I have given you readers out there an insight into the world of that loveable creature called the Aircraft Handler, or to give him his other more lovable nickname, Chockheads, with his strange brand of humour and that camaraderie. I hope it has given you some pleasures to read as it gave me to write them.

Also, I hope I have shown you through my eyes what I/we got up to back then. Remember that most of the incidents happened in the Sixties and early Seventies. I believe the reason we could get away with a lot more because political correctness and Health and Safety were just words, that is to say they could still discipline you if you did anything wrong, but they had to catch you first. We worked hard and played even harder.

I was officially discharged on January 12th 1989. From a personal point of view, if I had my time over again I would not change one day.

To close, I have been out of the mob for a few years and that mythical creature has followed me here. You know the one, that big black gorilla. Yes, he spends all your money, craps in your mouth and throws your clothes around the room.

"Nostris In Manibus Tuti"

The Future

I recently had the opportunity to visit HMS Ocean and I met her flight deck crew. The future looks bright and is in good hands. The camaraderie, sense of humour and their professionalism was reminiscent of days gone by.

Bill Korth, July 2013

Glossary

Air Traffic Softie	Aircraft Handler who works in Air Traffic
B.A.	Breathing apparatus
Barrack Stanchion	Rating who has not been to sea for years
Bee's Knees	Brilliant
Big E	Nickname of HMS Eagle
BMH	British Military Hospital
Booties	Royal Marines
Bowser	Water tanker vehicle
Bricks and Sticks	Ministry of Public Buildings & Works (DOE)
Bronzy-bronzy	Sunbathing
Buzz Bosun	Person who spreads rumours
Can spanner	Tin opener
Chacon	Large portable wooden storage area
Crusher	Naval Police
CPO	Chief Petty Officer
DATCO	Duty Air Traffic Officer
Dan Buoy	Location Beacon for downed aircraft
Dipped Out	Missing out
DTS	Dinner time session (drinking)
Draft Chit	Posting Form
Exped	Expedition, i.e. camping
FDOs	Flight Deck Officers

Fez	The Far East
FONAC	Flag Officer Naval Air Command
FO2FEF	Flag Officer in charge of Far East Fleet
Gollock	Large jungle knife
Green parrot	Helicopter, green in colour
Green slug	Sleeping bag, green in colour
Guzz	Name for Plymouth Naval Base
Hands to bath	To swim in the ocean whilst ship has stopped
Hangar rat	Aircraft Handler who works in the hangar
Heads	Toilets
Helo	Helicopter
Josh	Master-At-Arms
Killick	Leading Hand
Little F	Lt. Commander, second in charge of flying
Luppins	Money
Messdeck	Accommodation
Messmen	Cleaner of Senior Rates mess
MAOT	Mobile Air Operations Team
MOD plods	Ministry of Defence Police
Monsoon ditch	Ditches which run alongside Singaporean roads
MOB	Term used to refer to the Navy
Oggin	The ocean, the sea
Procedure Alpha	Upper deck ceremonial

PO	Petty Officer
Pussers	All things naval
RAN	Royal Australian Navy
RPOs	Regulating Petty Officers (Naval Police)
Roof Rat	Aircraft Handler working on the flight deck
Roughie Toughie	Aircraft Handler working on a fire station
Rupert	Officer
SATCO	Senior Air Traffic Control Officer
Sea Stories	To tell stories, same as *swing the lamp*
Shave off	Annoyed
F***g shave off**	Very annoyed
SLRs	Self-loading rifles
Stokers	Persons who work in the boiler room
Scrumpy Shufflers	Fire crew football team (Yeovilton)
Swing the lamp	To tell stories
Three-day camel hike	To take a long time to get anywhere
Tot	A measure of rum
VCP	Visual Control Position
Wings	Officer in charge of flying
Yonks	A long time
6 x 6	Six-wheeled drive fire vehicle
C130	RAF Hercules transport aircraft

Printed in Great Britain
by Amazon